"Where Wings Take Dream"

The Looking-Glass Logic of George W. Bush

M. Andrew Holowchak, Ph.D.

Kutztown University

ISBN 1-893157-16-4

Published by

BRIDGER HOUSE PUBLISHERS, INC

P.O. Box 2208, Carson City, NV 89702, USA

1-800-729-4131

Layout by therighttype.com

Printed in the United States of America

10 9 8 7 6 5 4 3 2 1

Dedication

This book is dedicated to my long-deceased maternal grandfather Michael Chemny, whose dreams were not so "trampled" as they might have seemed, and to my brother David.

Acknowledgements

I would like to thank Bridger House Publishers for their excellent and expeditious work on this project. I would also like to thank my students at Kutztown University this past year for their many fine comments.

Contents

Introduction

> Families is [*sic*] where our nation finds hope, where wings take dream.
>
> LaCrosse, WI, Oct. 18, 2000

In 1862, Charles Lutwidge Dodgson, better known as Lewis Carroll, wrote a story about a little girl named Alice, who, from boredom, followed a peculiar white rabbit, with pocket watch and waist coat, down a large rabbit-hole—mindless of where it would lead her. Falling on a heap of sticks and dried leaves, she found herself in a place called "Wonderland"—so queer and with such bizarre characters it defied conventional logic. It was a magical, yet mysterious place, where the oldest rule of a book did not have to be the first one, where people who were thirsty ate dry biscuits to quench their thirst, where one had to walk directly away from someone to get near to that person, and where the grin of a Cheshire cat could exist without the cat!

The intent of *"Where Wings Take Dream": The Looking-Glass Logic of George W. Bush* is not to rehash the story of Alice; it is rather to suggest that we, like poor Alice, have ourselves, since the election of George W. Bush as our president in 2000, followed a "rabbit" down a hole and found ourselves in a place so curious it too defies conventional logic. Since Bush's election, we too are living in a Wonderland of sorts, where preemptive killing is judged to be a viable mechanism to promote world peace; where presidential speeches need to be deciphered in every detail for their truth-content; where statistical data and facts are deemed irrelevant for claims; where every human life is proclaimed precious, but human lives take a back seat to political and economic agendas abroad; and where a leader elected by the people refuses to be answerable to them. This book, then, takes us into the mind of George W. Bush. Specifically, it is a look at the reasoning abilities or "logic" of George W. Bush.

Logic is, of course, inextricably linked with language. The president's difficulties with language have now been well documented and are the subject of several fine books in the last few years. To the best of my knowledge, no one has yet to look exclusively at Bush's use and, what is more often the case, *misuse* of logic. This book is, then, an attempt to supplement the existing literature.

The first part of *"Where Wings Take Dream"* examines Bush's political and ethical rhetoric. The first three chapters focus on political rhetoric. Chapter 1, "America at War", begins with Bush's response to the tragic events of 9/11 and then walk readers through the wars with Afghanistan and Iraq. Chapter 2 is "The Bush Doctrine"—which comprises liberalism, preemption, unilateralism, and what I call his *Officium Paci* doctrine (his unique notion of what a "just peace" entails). The third chapter covers various political miscellanea—Bush's thoughts on America, terrorism, religion, and education. Chapters 4 and 5 comprise Bush's ethical rhetoric. Chapter 4 is entitled "Bush and Other-Concern" and covers Bush's uncanny ability to flip-flop between moral absolutism and moral consequentialism as well as his views on values, moral clarity, culpability, the ethics of war, and the environment. Chapter 5, "'Know Thyself'", comprises Bush's views on himself, leadership, being son of George H. W. Bush, his avowed dyslexia and substance abuse, compassionate conservatism, unifying America and Congress, and progressivism.

The second part is an analysis of the "elements" of Bush's looking-glass logic. Chapters 6 through 9 examine the various rhetorical devices the president uses, consciously or unconsciously, to enable him to stay afloat in a world of endless challenges, most of which are consequences of his own duplicity. These rules are *Keep your "adversary" off-guard* (chapter 6) *Never take a blow straight-on* (chapter 7), *Confuse or tire out your "adversary"* (chapter 8), and, when everything else fails, *Express your confusion unbashedly* (chapter 9). Here each rule is amply illustrated through specific rhetorical tactics, many of which are logical fallacies, such as appeals to fear, *ad hominem,* slanting, false appeals to authority, *non sequitur*, and equivocation. The final section, chapters 10 to 13, ends appropriately enough with an A-to-Z analysis of Bush's difficulties with constructing and articulating meaningful sentences. The argument here is that many of the difficulties the president has in public situations result from a more fundamental problem: cognitive impairment at what is often called the "atomic" level of reasoning. Put simply, one ought not to expect superb reasoning skills from one who cannot string sentences together correctly.

Overall, *"Where Wings Take Dream"* is not a book that aims directly to be critical of Bush's political and moral agendas. Moreover, it is not a book that aims directly to be critical of Bush the man. This is a book that focuses on Bush's unique thinking—his looking-glass logic—and the confusion in his political and moral agendas, I hope to show, are mere byproducts of a deep-rooted ratiocinative confusion in the man. Thus, I include many significant chunks of text and statements from interviews, speeches, and formal and informal addresses to demonstrate this point.

The material will, of course, reflect my own biases of selection and what I have selected, I freely admit, tends to focus on Bush at his worst. I offer up no apologies for this. One would expect the world's most powerful and prominent leader and diplomat to be a skilful, articulate, and persuasive orator, a masterful dialectician, and a clear thinker. Put bluntly, this would seem to be part of job description. Nonetheless, Bush's debates, addresses, and press conferences show the president to be anything but skilful, articulate, masterful, clear, or persuasive. This ought to have caused outrage, even panic, among the American public at large as it has done worldwide. Astonishingly, it hasn't. This book is admittedly, like many others, a humble effort to create outrage at large. Without such outrage, we can only hope that each of us, at the end of Bush's second term, will wake and say, as did young Alice, "Oh, I've had such a curious dream!" Of course, "curious" is not quite the right word!

PART ONE
DOWN THE RABBIT HOLE

SECTION ONE
BUSH'S POLITICAL RHETORIC

> "Our nation's cause has always been larger than our nation's defense. We fight, as we always fight, for a just peace—a peace that favors human liberty".
>
> George W. Bush

THE MONTHS OF GEORGE W. BUSH'S PRESIDENCY PRIOR to 9/11 were unremarkable. Forty-two percent of the first seven months was spent away from the White House. Much of this away time was spent fly-fishing, running, working the land, or even doing a bit of executive work at his Prairie Chapel Ranch in Crawford, Texas. "[W]hen I'm not in Washington", said Bush, "there's a pretty good chance you'll find me on our place in Crawford, Texas".[1] Since being elected president, Bush has spent so much time at his ranch in Texas that it is now called the "Western White House" or the "Texas White House". Everything was running fairly smoothly till 9/11.

---

1 http://austin.about.com/cs/bushbiographies/a/crawford_ranch.htm.

On September 11 of 2001, as documented by filmmaker Michael Moore in "Fahrenheit 9/11", Bush sat quietly in a Florida classroom of Emma Booker Elementary School, while moments earlier in New York, a plane flew into one of the two buildings of the Twin Towers. On receiving news of the second tower being hit, the president—frozen by indecision and panic—grabbed a nearby book, *My Pet Goat*, and sat motionless for many minutes while gazing blankly into the book. There was the same look on his face that one might expect of a panicky child, trapped by indecision brought about by a radical change of his environment. It's difficult to say what was going on in the Bush's head, when the country was being besieged. Was he so completely frozen by panic that he couldn't think at all? After many minutes of indecision, the president finally addressed the school and left.

It is here that our story begins….

Chapter 1
America at War

> *"'Off with his head!' or 'Off with her head!' about once in a minute. Alice began to feel very uneasy: to be sure, she had not as yet had any dispute with the Queen, but she knew that it might happen any minute, 'and then', thought she, 'what would become of me? They're dreadfully fond of beheading people here: the great wonder is, that there's any one left alive!'"*

9/11 and Its Aftermath

After the attacks on 9-11, for much of the day, the president was nowhere to be found. As the story is told today, he was being flown around from place to place to ensure his safety. When he finally did get a chance to address the nation at Barksdale Air Force Base in Louisiana, he said briefly:

> Freedom itself was attacked this morning by a faceless coward. And freedom will be defended. I want to reassure the American people that the full resources of the federal government are working to assist local authorities to save lives and to help the victims of these attacks. Make no mistake, the United States will hunt down and punish those responsible for these cowardly acts. I've been in regular contact with the Vice President, Secretary of Defense, the national security team, and my cab-

> inet. We have taken all appropriate security precautions to protect the American people. Our military at home and around the world is on high alert status. And we have taken the necessary security precautions to continue the functions of your government. We have been in touch with leaders of Congress and with world leaders to assure them that we will do whatever is necessary to protect America and Americans. I ask the American people to join me in saying a "thanks" for all the folks who have been fighting hard to rescue our fellow citizens, and to join me in saying a prayer for the victims and their families. The resolve of our great nation is being tested, but make no mistake. We will show the world that we will pass this test. God bless.

Finally at 8:30 pm, the president formally addressed a panicky and terrified nation. It was the first of numerous speeches that explained the attack as an attack on America's freedom. The freedom-vs.-fear, good-vs.-evil, and peace-and-security-vs.-terror-and-chaos themes were born.

> Good evening. Today, our fellow citizens, our way of life, our very freedom came under attack in a series of deliberate and deadly terrorist acts.... Thousands of lives were suddenly ended by evil, despicable acts of terror.... These acts of mass murder were intended to frighten our nation into chaos and retreat. But they have failed.
>
> Our country is strong. A great people has [*sic*] been moved to defend a great nation. Terrorist attacks can shake the foundations of our biggest buildings, but they cannot touch the foundation of America. These acts shatter steel, but they cannot dent the steel of American resolve. America was targeted for attack because we're the brightest beacon for freedom and opportunity in the world. And no one will keep that light from shining.
>
> Today, our nation saw evil—the very worst of human nature—and we responded with the best of America. With the daring of our rescue workers, with the caring for strangers and neighbors who came to give blood and help in any way they could....
>
> The search is underway for those who were behind these evil acts. I have directed the full resources of our intelligence and law enforcement communities to find those responsible and to bring them to justice. We will make no distinction between the terrorists who committed these acts and those who harbor them.... America and our friends and allies join with all those who want peace and security in the world, and we stand together to win the war against terrorism.

> Tonight, I ask for your prayers for all those who grieve, for the children whose worlds have been shattered, for all whose sense of safety and security has been threatened. And I pray they will be comforted by a Power greater than any of us, spoken through the ages in Psalm 23: "Even though I walk through the valley of the shadow of death, I fear no evil for you are with me". This is a day when all Americans from every walk of life unite in our resolve for justice and peace. America has stood down enemies before, and we will do so this time. None of us will ever forget this day, yet we go forward to defend freedom and all that is good and just in our world. Thank you. Good night. And God bless America.

Bush raised the rhetoric a notch the following day. These were not mere acts of terror, these were "acts of war" that were directed not merely against America, but what America, more than any other nation, stands for—freedom and democracy.

> The deliberate and deadly attacks, which were carried out yesterday against our country, were more than acts of terror. They were acts of war. This will require our country to unite in steadfast determination and resolve. Freedom and democracy are under attack.

Many experts agree that the events of 9/11 gave Bush an identity as president that hitherto he did not have. Before 9/11, in a strange sort of way, the world was overwhelmingly complex. Bush had to concern himself with committing to memory the names of leaders of nations that he did not quite know and getting the names of multi-syllabic countries right. The atrocities of 9/11 gave Bush what he had been without for months—recognition and validation as a world leader.

Unfortunately, 9/11 also gave Bush something immeasurably more dangerous—presidential power without responsibility for its abuse. The events of 9/11 were not only the motive for the campaign in Afghanistan, which was conducted with a large amount of global sympathy, but also a motive to invade Iraq—a country both rich in oil and led by "the guy who tried to kill my dad". Because of 9/11, for the first time in decades, Americans were genuinely afraid. Bush would monitor, adjust, and play on their fears to justify an invasion of Iraq—a country which had nothing to do with 9/11—as well as his reelection campaign in 2004.

Because of 9/11, the world had changed and so the rules of the game had to change with it.

> The world *changed* on September the 11th. Obviously, it *changed* for thousands of people's lives for whom we still mourn. But it *changed* for America, and it's very important that the American people understand the *change*. We are now a battle ground. We are vulnerable. Therefore, we cannot ignore gathering threats across the ocean. It used to be that we could pick or choose whether or not we would become involved. If we saw a threat, it may be a threat to a friend, in which case we would be involved, but never did we realize the threat could be directed at the American people.
>
> And that *changed*. And therefore, when we hear of stories about weapons of mass destruction in the hands of a brutal dictator, who hates America, we need to take that seriously, and we are. And when we find out there's links between Baghdad and a killer who actually ordered the killing of one of our fellow citizens, we've got to realize the—what that means to our future. And that's why this administration and this country is [*sic*] holding the U.N. Security Council and the world to its demands that Saddam Hussein disarm.
>
> White Sulphur Springs, WV, Feb. 9, 2003

The pathway to security was stated as preemptively eliminating all "gathering threats" to the United States before they could fully materialize.

Today, the events of 9/11 continually creep up in press conferences abroad, in an effort for Bush to justify America's preemption in Iraq and win global sympathy for our continued occupation of it. During a visit to Mainz, Germany, on February 23 of 2005, Bush he replied to a young German woman, who asked him about American dependence on oil and its impact on the U.S.'s relationship with Russia, by turning back to 9/11.

> That's an interesting question. The foreign policy of our country for years—I'm stepping back, I'm kind of going to branch out from Russia, and I'll get back to Russia.... And let me say something about September the 11th. I think this will help frame the conversation as we

> go forward. For some, September the 11th was a passing moment in history. In other words, it was a terrible moment, but it passes. For me, and my government, and many in the United States, it permanently changed our outlook on the world. Those two attitudes caused us, sometimes, to talk past each other, and I plead guilty at times. But as this conversation goes on, I want you to remember that point of view. As a result of feeling like—that my main obligation is now to protect the American people, and to confront an ideology of hate. We are no longer—our primary objective is the spread of freedom.

This reply illustrates two things. First, it shows the continued tendency of Bush to speak of 9/11 as an irreversible turning point in American history that justifies what might otherwise appear to be inappropriate and vicious U.S. actions. Second, it shows another tendency of Bush: If he's unhappy or uncomfortable talking about something, he doesn't talk about it.

The War in Afghanistan

After the horrific events of 9/11, in a formal address to the country on September 20 of 2001, Bush offered the following threat to members of the terrorist group, al Qaeda.

> And tonight, the United States of America makes the following demands on the Taliban: Deliver to United States authorities all the leaders of al Qaeda who hide in your land. Release all foreign nationals, including American citizens, you have unjustly imprisoned. Protect foreign journalists, diplomats and aid workers in your country. Close immediately and permanently every terrorist training camp in Afghanistan, and hand over every terrorist, and every person in their support structure, to appropriate authorities. Give the United States full access to terrorist training camps, so we can make sure they are no longer operating. These demands are not open to negotiation or discussion. The Taliban must act, and act immediately. They will hand over the terrorists, or they will share in their fate.

The threats were not heeded and, on October 7 of 2001, the president formally announced that operation "Enduring Freedom" was underway in Afghanistan.

> This military action is a part of our campaign against terrorism, another front in a war that has already been joined through diplomacy, intelligence, the freezing of financial assets, and the arrests of known terrorists by law enforcement agents in 38 countries. Given the nature and reach of our enemies, we will win this conflict by the patient accumulation of successes, by meeting a series of challenges with determination and will and purpose.
>
> Today we focus on Afghanistan, but the battle is broader. Every nation has a choice to make. In this conflict, there is no neutral ground. If any government sponsors the outlaws and killers of innocents, they have become outlaws and murderers, themselves. And they will take that lonely path at their own peril.
>
> I'm speaking to you today from the Treaty Room of the White House, a place where American Presidents have worked for peace. We're a peaceful nation. Yet, as we have learned, so suddenly and so tragically, there can be no peace in a world of sudden terror. In the face of today's new threat, the only way to pursue peace is to pursue those who threaten it.
>
> We did not ask for this mission, but we will fulfill it. The name of today's military operation is Enduring Freedom. We defend not only our precious freedoms, but also the freedom of people everywhere to live and raise their children free from fear.

Behind the invasion of Afghanistan is a principle, introduced on 9/11, that would become a prominent theme of later addresses: All who sponsor terrorists or offer them sanctuary are themselves terrorists, what might be called the *Identity of Bedfellows Principle*. For instance, on October 30 of 2001, Bush said:

> I also want to make it clear that the doctrine I laid out to the United States Congress is a doctrine this nation will enforce. It says clearly that *if you harbor a terrorist, if you feed a terrorist, if you provide sanctuary to a terrorist, if you fund a terrorist, you are just as guilty as the terrorist that inflicted the harm on the American people.*

One month later, Bush would add in an address to the United Nations:

> The Taliban are now learning this lesson—*that regime and the terrorists who support it are now virtually indistinguishable.* Together they

> promote terror abroad and impose a reign of terror on the Afghan people. Women are executed in Kabal's soccer stadium. They can be beaten for wearing socks that are too thin. Men are jailed for missing prayer meetings.
>
> The United States, supported by many nations, is bringing justice to the terrorists in Afghanistan. We're making progress against military targets, and that is our objective. Unlike the enemy, we seek to minimize, not maximize, the loss of innocent life....
>
> I make this promise to all the victims of that regime: The Taliban's days of harboring terrorists and dealing in heroin and brutalizing women are drawing to a close. And when that regime is gone, the people of Afghanistan will say with the rest of the world: "good riddance".
>
> I can promise, too, that America will join the world in helping the people of Afghanistan rebuild their country.
>
> Nov. 10, 2001

The pledge to rebuild the county was soon swept under the rug. Money and the military were now needed for another agenda. America turned its sights toward Iraq and the elimination of Saddam Hussein. They justification for this new agenda would be to claim that there was a link between Hussein and the events of 9/11.

In the month after his address to the United Nations, with all that had happened to the American people since 9/11, Bush had the temerity and insensitivity to sum the year thus:

> But all in all, it's been a fabulous year for Laura and me.
>
> Dec. 21, 2001

The War in Iraq

Why War?

All too soon, Bush turned away from helping the people of Afghanistan rebuild their war-torn country and turned his full attention to an old and familiar enemy—Saddam Hussein. Hussein was said to be a "gathering threat" to global securing that needed immediate attention.

> [T]he world is a dangerous place, particularly with people like Saddam Hussein in power.
>
> Saddam Hussein is a man who told the world he wouldn't have weapons of mass destruction, but he's got them. He's a man who a while ago who was close to having a nuclear weapon. Imagine if this madman had a nuclear weapon. It's a man who not only has chemical weapons, but he's used chemical weapons against some of his neighbors. He used chemical weapons, incredibly enough, against his own people. He can't stand America. He can't stand some of our closest friends.
>
> Apr. 30, 2002

Almost a year after the events of 9/11, Bush addressed the United Nations about physical evidence of this "grave and gathering threat".

> Right now, Iraq is expanding and improving facilities that were used for the production of biological weapons. United Nations' inspections also revealed that Iraq likely maintains stockpiles of VX, mustard and other chemical agents, and that the regime is rebuilding and expanding facilities capable of producing chemical weapons. And in 1995, after four years of deception, Iraq finally admitted it had a crash nuclear weapons program prior to the Gulf War.
>
> We know now, were it not for that war, the regime in Iraq would likely have possessed a nuclear weapon no later than 1993. Today, Iraq continues to withhold important information about its nuclear program—weapons design, procurement logs, experiment data, an accounting of nuclear materials and documentation of foreign assistance. Iraq employs capable nuclear scientists and technicians. It retains physical infrastructure needed to build a nuclear weapon. Iraq has made several attempts to buy high-strength aluminum tubes used to enrich uranium for a nuclear weapon. Should Iraq acquire fissile material, it would be able to build a nuclear weapon within a year. And Iraq's state-controlled media has reported numerous meetings between Saddam Hussein and his nuclear scientists, leaving little doubt about his continued appetite for these weapons....
>
> We know that Saddam Hussein pursued weapons of mass murder even when inspectors were in his country. Are we to assume that he stopped when they left? *The history, the logic, and the facts lead to one conclusion: Saddam Hussein's regime is a grave and gathering danger.* To suggest otherwise is to hope against the evidence. To assume this regime's good faith is to bet the lives of millions and the peace of the world in a reckless gamble. And this is a risk we must not take....

> My nation will work with the U.N. Security Council to meet our common challenge. If Iraq's regime defies us again, the world must move deliberately, decisively to hold Iraq to account. We will work with the U.N. Security Council for the necessary resolutions. *But the purposes of the United States should not be doubted. The Security Council resolutions will be enforced—the just demands of peace and security will be met—or action will be unavoidable. And a regime that has lost its legitimacy will also lose its power.*
>
> Sept. 12, 2002

On October 7 of 2002, Bush asserted that he knew Hussein had weapons of mass destruction (hereafter, WMDs). He added that this "knowledge" was a sufficient justification for preemptive action in the interest of American and global security.

> If we know Saddam Hussein has dangerous weapons today—*and we do*—does it make any sense for the world to wait to confront him as he grows even stronger and develops even more dangerous weapons?...
>
> And surveillance photos reveal that the regime is rebuilding facilities that it had used to produce chemical and biological weapons. Every chemical and biological weapon that Iraq has or makes is a direct violation of the truce that ended the Persian Gulf War in 1991. Yet, Saddam Hussein has chosen to build and keep these weapons despite international sanctions, U.N. demands, and isolation from the civilized world....
>
> *Knowing* these realities, America must not ignore the threat gathering against us. Facing clear evidence of peril, *we cannot wait for the final proof—the smoking gun—that could come in the form of a mushroom cloud.*

In his State of the Union Address on Jan. 28 of 2003, Bush reassured the American people of the gathering and grave threat. He also threatened to lead a coalition to disarm Hussein in the event that Hussein would not willfully disarm.

> U.S. intelligence indicates that Saddam Hussein had upwards of 30,000 munitions capable of delivering chemical agents. Inspectors recently turned up 16 of them—despite Iraq's recent declaration denying their existence. Saddam Hussein has not accounted for the remaining 29,984 of these prohibited munitions. He's given no evidence that he has destroyed them. From three Iraqi defectors we know that Iraq, in the late 1990s, had several mobile biological weapons labs. These are designed to produce germ warfare agents, and can be moved from place

> to a place to evade inspectors. Saddam Hussein has not disclosed these facilities. He's given no evidence that he has destroyed them....
>
> We will consult. But let there be no misunderstanding: *If Saddam Hussein does not fully disarm, for the safety of our people and for the peace of the world, we will lead a coalition to disarm him.*

Yet this was not enough. On February 9 of 2003, from an address from White Sulphur Springs, West Virginia, the president openly threatened the authority of the United Nations itself. Astonishingly, the United Nations, like Afghanistan (and Iraq later), was given an ultimatum: Either jump on the bandwagon for war or become irrelevant.

> And it's a moment of truth for the United Nations. *The United Nations gets to decide, shortly, whether or not it is going to be relevant, in terms of keeping the peace, whether or not its words mean anything.* But one thing is certain, for the sake of peace and for the sake of security, the United States and our friends and allies, we will disarm Saddam Hussein if he will not disarm himself.

Members of the United Nations—even friends and long-time allies—were not in the least amused.

On March 17 of 2003, Bush addressed the American public with more rhetoric, playing on American fear, concerning the gathering and grave threat in Iraq.

> The danger is clear: using chemical, biological or, one day, nuclear weapons, obtained with the help of Iraq, the terrorists could fulfill their stated ambitions and kill thousands or hundreds of thousands of innocent people in our country, or any other....
>
> We are now acting because the risks of inaction would be far greater. In one year, or five years, the power of Iraq to inflict harm on all free nations would be multiplied many times over. With these capabilities, Saddam Hussein and his terrorist allies could choose the moment of deadly conflict when they are strongest. We choose to meet that threat now, where it arises, before it can appear suddenly in our skies and cities.

The argument from fear won the day and the hearts and souls of the American people. Two days later, with full support of the U.S. Congress, U.S. troops invaded Iraq.

> My fellow citizens, at this hour, American and coalition forces are in the early stages of military operations to disarm Iraq, to free its people and to defend the world from grave danger....
>
> Mar. 19, 2003

Though members of Congress were foursquare behind the president, tens of thousands of people from all over the globe angrily protested the U.S. invasion.

The Controversy over WMDs

President Bush, on May 1 of 2003, landed aboard the USS Abraham Lincoln on a fighter plane to declare, in effect, that the war with Iraq was over. Decked out in a full flight suit, he looked every bit a manly, take-charge president. When the appropriate number of photos was taken, he took off the flight suit and gave the following address. I include here only the introductory comments.

> Thank you all very much. Admiral Kelly, Captain Card, officers and sailors of the USS Abraham Lincoln, my fellow Americans: *Major combat operations in Iraq have ended.* In the battle of Iraq, *the United States and our allies have prevailed. And now our coalition is engaged in securing and reconstructing that country.*
>
> In this battle, we have fought for the cause of liberty, and for the peace of the world. Our nation and our coalition are proud of this accomplishment, yet it is you, the members of the United States military, who achieved it. Your courage, your willingness to face danger for your country and for each other, made this day possible. Because of you, our nation is more secure. Because of you, *the tyrant has fallen, and Iraq is free.*
>
> Operation Iraqi Freedom was carried out with *a combination of precision and speed and boldness the enemy did not expect, and the world*

> *had not seen before.* From distant bases or ships at sea, we sent planes and missiles that could destroy an enemy division, or strike a single bunker. Marines and soldiers charged to Baghdad across 350 miles of hostile ground, in *one of the swiftest advances of heavy arms in history.* You have shown the world the skill and the might of the American Armed Forces.
>
> May 1, 2003

The pageantry of the speech is evident. It focuses not merely on results, but results of a specific kind: swift, precise, bold, and efficient.

Yet behind the façade of America's swift victory were the mounting U.S. and civilian casualties as a result of continued terrorist attacks after the U.S. "victory". More than this, there came to the attention of journalists that Bush's administration was not truthful about its real motivation for war with Iraq. For one, WMDs were never found and, when Bush gave up its search for them, he changed his tune about his reasons for the invasion in the first place. He acknowledged that the intelligence behind his statement that Iraq had WMDs was faulty, but he added that this was never really the reason for the invasion of Iraq. Hussein's *potential* to build such weapons was the real reason for going to war.

Many members of Congress, the press, and the American public were not so readily convinced. They asked Bush minimally for some admission of wrongdoing. None was forthcoming. Consider, for instance, this lengthy but revealing exchange between Bush and Tim Russert on NBC's *Meet the Press* on February 7 of 2004.

> Russert: The night you took the country to war, March 17th, you said this: "Intelligence gathered by this and other governments leaves no doubt that the Iraq regime continues to possess and conceal some of the most lethal weapons ever devised".
>
> Bush: Right. Correct.
>
> Russert: How do you respond to critics who say that you brought the nation to war under false pretenses?

Bush: Yes. First of all, I expected to find the weapons. Sitting behind this desk making a very difficult decision of war and peace, and I based my decision on the best intelligence possible, intelligence that had been gathered over the years, intelligence that not only our analysts thought was valid but analysts from other countries thought were valid. And I made a decision based upon that intelligence in the context of the war against terror. In other words, we were attacked, and therefore every threat had to be reanalyzed. Every threat had to be looked at. Every *potential* harm to America had to be judged in the context of this war on terror. And I made the decision, obviously, to take our case to the international community in the hopes that we could do this—achieve a disarmament of Saddam Hussein peacefully. In other words, we looked at the intelligence. And we remembered the fact that he had used weapons, which meant he had had weapons. We knew the fact that he was paying for suicide bombers. We knew the fact he was funding terrorist groups. In other words, he was a dangerous man. And that was the intelligence I was using prior to the run up to this war. Now, let me—which is — this is a vital question—

Russert: Nothing more important.

Bush: Vital question. And so we—I expected there to be stockpiles of weapons. But David Kay has found the *capacity* to produce weapons. Now, when David Kay goes in and says we haven't found stockpiles yet, and there's theories [*sic*] as to where the weapons went. They could have been destroyed during the war. Saddam and his henchmen could have destroyed them as we entered into Iraq. They could be hidden. They could have been transported to another country, and we'll find out. That's what the Iraqi Survey Group—let me—let me finish here. But David Kay did report to the American people that Saddam had the capacity to make weapons. Saddam Hussein was dangerous with weapons. Saddam Hussein was dangerous with the *ability* to make weapons. He was a dangerous man in the dangerous part of the world.

And I made the decision to go to the United Nations. By the way, quoting a lot of their data—in other words, this is unaccounted for stockpiles that you thought he had because I don't think America can stand by and hope for the best from a madman, and I believe it is essential—I believe it is essential—that when we see a threat, we deal with those threats before they become imminent. It's too late if they become imminent. It's too late in this new kind of war, and so that's why I made the decision I made.

Russert: Mr. President, the Director of the CIA said that his briefings had qualifiers and caveats, but when you spoke to the country, you said "there is no doubt". When Vice President Cheney spoke to the country, he said "there is no doubt". Secretary Powell, "no doubt". Secretary Rumsfeld, "no doubt, we know where the weapons are". You said, quote, "The Iraqi regime is a threat of unique urgency". "Saddam Hussein is a threat that we must deal with as quickly as possible". You gave the clear sense that this was an immediate threat that must be dealt with.

Bush: I think, if I might remind you that in my language I called it a "grave and gathering threat", but I don't want to get into word contests. But what I do want to share with you is my sentiment at the time. There was no doubt in my mind that Saddam Hussein was a danger to America. No doubt.

Russert: In what way?

Bush: Well, because he had the *capacity* to have a weapon, make a weapon. We thought he had weapons. The international community thought he had weapons. But he had the *capacity to make a weapon* and then let that weapon fall into the hands of a shadowy terrorist network. It's important for people to understand the context in which I made a decision here in the Oval Office. I'm dealing with a world in which we have gotten struck by terrorists with airplanes, and we get intelligence saying that there is you know—we want to harm America. And the worst nightmare scenario for any president is to realize that these kind [*sic*] of terrorist networks had the capacity to arm up with some of these deadly weapons, and then strike us. And the President of the United States' most solemn responsibility is to keep this country secure. And the man was a threat, and we dealt with him, and we dealt with him because we cannot hope for the best. We can't say, "Let's don't deal with Saddam Hussein. Let's hope he changes his stripes, or let's trust in the goodwill of Saddam Hussein. Let's, let us, kind of, try to contain him". Containment doesn't work with a man who is a madman. And remember, Tim, he had used weapons against his own people.

Russert: But can you launch a pre-emptive war without iron-clad, absolute intelligence that he had weapons of mass destruction?

Bush: Let me take a step back for a second and—there is no such thing necessarily *in a dictatorial regime* [oops!] of iron-clad absolutely solid evidence. The evidence I had was the best possible evidence that he had a weapon.

Russert: But it may have been wrong.

Bush: Well, but what wasn't wrong was the fact that he had the *ability* to make a weapon. That wasn't right.

Russert: This is an important point because when you say that he has biological and chemical weapons and unmanned aerial vehicles—

Bush: —which he had.

Russert: —and they could come and attack the United States, you're saying to the American people: we have to deal now with a man who has these things.

Bush: That's exactly what I said.

Russert: And if that's not the case, do you believe if you had gone to the Congress and said he should be removed because he's a threat to his people but I'm not sure he has weapons of mass destruction, Congress would authorize war?

Bush: I went to Congress with the same intelligence—Congress saw the same intelligence I had, and they looked at exactly what I looked at, and they made an informed judgment based upon the information that I had. The same information, by the way, that my predecessor had. And all of us, you know, made this judgment that Saddam Hussein needed to be removed. You mentioned "pre-emption". If I might, I went to the United Nations and said, "Here is what we know, you know, at this moment, and you need to act. After all, you are the body that issued resolution after resolution after resolution, and he ignored those resolutions". So, in other words, when you say "pre-emption", it almost sounds like, "Well, Mr. President, you decided to move". What I decided to do was to go to the international community and see if we could not disarm Saddam Hussein peacefully through international pressure. You remember U.N. Security Council Resolution 1441 clearly stated "show us your arms and destroy them, or your programs and destroy them". And we said, "There are serious consequences if you don't" and that was a unanimous verdict. In

> other words, the worlds [*sic*] of the U.N. Security Council said, "We're unanimous and you're a danger". So, it wasn't just me and the United States. The world thought he was dangerous and needed to be disarmed. And, of course, he defied the world once again.
>
> In my judgment, when the United States says, "There will be serious consequences" [*sic*], and if there isn't serious consequences it creates adverse consequences. People look at us and say, "They don't mean what they say. They are not willing to follow through".
>
> And by the way, by clearly stating policy, whether it be in Afghanistan or stating the policy that we expect you, Mr. Saddam Hussein, to disarm, your choice to disarm, but if you don't, there will be serious consequences in following through, it has had positive effects in the world. Libya, for example, there was an positive effect in Libya where Moammar Khaddafy voluntarily disclosed his weapons programs and agreed to dismantle—dismantle them, and the world is a better place as a result of that. And the world is a safer and better place as a result of Saddam Hussein not being in power.
>
> *Meet the Press,* Feb. 7, 2004

In a telephone interview with Rush Limbaugh, Bush had this to say about the warrant for the invasion of Iraq.

> Now, Iraq. You see, one of the lessons of September the 11th is that we gotta deal with threats before they fully materialize, and we saw a threat in Iraq. I say "we". The Congress saw a threat, I saw a threat and the United Nations Security Council saw a threat. In other words, the world took a look and said, "Saddam is a threat", and here's why they thought he was a threat.
>
> One, he used weapons of mass destruction, and one of the most dangerous parts of this new war is that if the enemy were ever to acquire the *capacity* to use a weapon of mass destruction it would make September 11th, you know, pale in comparison, and so we saw that threat.
>
> Secondly, he had ties to terrorists. Abu Nidal was housed in Iraq, his organization. He was the guy that killed Leon Klinghoffer. He was a known terrorist. Zarqawi—who's now, you know, the person beheading people in Iraq today—was in and out of Baghdad and Iraq, as were members of his organization. So he had terrorist ties. As a matter of fact,

> not only did he have terrorist ties, he used to subsidize families of these suicide bombers, which is a terrorist act.
>
> Thirdly, he invaded his neighbors. Fourthly, he was an enemy of this country, and we had been to war with him once. He had invaded others in the neighborhood. He was a source of great instability.
>
> So I saw a threat, and given the lessons of September the 11th, we decided to remove him from power, having tried diplomacy. See, I think it's very important for your listeners to know, Rush, that the commander-in-chief ought to try all avenues of diplomacy prior to committing troops and we did that. And so I'm sitting in the Oval Office, and I've seen a threat. I now see that he's ignoring the demands of the free world, he had no intention of disarming, as a matter of fact was systematically deceiving inspectors, and so I made the decision, a very difficult decision.
>
> Aug. 31, 2004

There were also some significant exchanges between Bush and Kerry on the issue of Iraq's supposed WMDs in their debates. First, there was the debate of September 30 of 2004 where Bush, through his grave-and-gathering threat argument, offered some additional ends-justify-the-means reasons for the invasion.

> A free Iraq will be an ally in the war on terror, and that's essential. A free Iraq will set a powerful example in the part of the world that is desperate for freedom. A free Iraq will help secure Israel. A free Iraq will enforce the hopes and aspirations of the reformers in places like Iran. A free Iraq is essential for the security of this country.

In their second debate on October 8 of 2004, Bush even gave the varied threats that Hussein was perceived to pose different labels.

> We all thought there was weapons [*sic*] there, Robin. My opponent thought there was weapons [*sic*] there. That's why he called him a *grave* threat. I wasn't happy when we found out there wasn't weapons [*sic*], and we've got an intelligence group together to figure out why. But Saddam Hussein was a *unique* threat. And the world is better off without him in power. And my opponent's plans lead me to conclude that Saddam Hussein would still be in power, and the world would be more dangerous.

When Hussein was believed by everyone to have WMDs, he was considered a "grave" threat. So, the U.S. went to war. When no weapons were found, the war was still justified, because Hussein, no longer a grave threat, was now a "unique" threat—presumably because he still had some unspecified capacity to build them at some future time. Either way however, the invasion was justified, as "the world is a better off without Saddam Hussein in power".

Bush argued in similar fashion in an interview with Diane Sawyer on December 16 of 2003. Frustrated with Sawyer's persistence on the issue of WMDs, Bush explained what he meant by a "gathering threat".

> Sawyer: But stated as a hard fact, that there were weapons of mass destruction as opposed to the possibility that he could move to acquire those weapons still.
> Bush: So what's the difference?
> Sawyer: Well—
> Bush: *The possibility that he could acquire weapons. If he were to acquire weapons, he would be the danger.* That's—that's what I'm trying to explain to you. A *gathering threat*, after 9/11, *is a threat that needed to be dealt with.* And it was done after 12 long years of the world saying the man's a danger. And so, we got rid of him. And there's no doubt the world is a safer, freer place as a result of Saddam being gone.

A "gathering threat", she is finally told, is "a threat that needed to be dealt with". And I suppose, if pressed further about just what "a threat that needed to be dealt with" is, Sawyer would have heard "a gathering threat".

Bush, of course, covered himself in this same interview by giving the discussion a moral twist:

> But on the big questions, about whether or not we should have gone into Afghanistan, the big question about whether we should have removed somebody in Iraq, I'll stand by those decisions, because I think they're right. That's really what you're—when they ask about the mistakes, that's what they're talking about. They're trying to say, "Did you make

> a mistake going into Iraq?" And the answer is, *"Absolutely not". It was the right decision.* The Duelfer report confirmed that decision today, because what Saddam Hussein was doing was trying to get rid of sanctions so he could reconstitute a weapons program. And the biggest threat facing America is terrorists with weapons of mass destruction. We knew he hated us. We knew he'd been—invaded other countries. We knew he tortured his own people.

These exchanges are, I believe, sufficient to show a shocking tendency of Bush: his decision-making invulnerability. No matter what evidence comes up concerning his decision to invade Iraq, he obstinately refuses to consider the possibility of having made a mistake—a narrow and terrifying attitude for one who is the president of the United States.

Today, there is mounting evidence to show that Bush did not go to war with Iraq because of WMDs. I list merely some of the concerns. First, Bush wanted to get, dead or alive and for whatever reason,[1] his father's nemesis in Gulf War I (and the man the United States supported with helicopters and materials for biological weapons when they were at war with Iran in the 1980s). According to a report in *Time* magazine, in March of 2002, about a year before the invasion of Iraq, Bush poked his head into a White House meeting between Condoleezza Rice, National Security Advisor, and three U.S. senators, who were discussing Iraq. According to the report, Bush said tersely, "Fuck Saddam, we're taking him out!"[2] And, of course, it is no accident that key members of the administration—Vice-President Dick Cheney, Deputy Secretary of Defense Paul Wolfowitz, Secretary of Defense Donald Rumsfeld, Undersecretary of State Richard Armitage, U.S. Ambassador to Iraq Zalmay Khalilzad, Richard Perle, and the president's brother Jeb Bush—are members of the proactive neoconservative group, Project for a New American

---

1 See Frank for a psychoanalytic analysis of possible tensions between Bush and his father. Justin A. Frank, *Bush on the Couch* (New York: ReganBooks, 2004), 141-161.

2 *Time*, March 23, 2003.

Century, which advocates strong military action in the world to promote American interests, values, and economic principles. Though the group was founded in 1997, neoconservatives have had their eyes on Iraq since the 1980s. In 1998, they drafted a letter to then-president Clinton, signed most notably by Rumsfeld and Wolfowitz, which called for the removal of Hussein. Oil, of course, comes into play significantly. An energy report, released in July of 2001 by Cheney, argued that the Middle East would produce 54 to 67 percent of the world's oil by 2020 and "the best way to reduce vulnerability is to open up areas of their energy sectors to foreign investment".[3] Cheney, of course, was hinting that these oil reserves could come under control of someone like Hussein, if the United States did not move proactively to secure the best interests of American companies. Moreover, this would certainly diminish America's dependence on OPEC. Finally, a memo from Tony Blair's staff—called the Downing Street Memo—states that "intelligence and facts [concerning the war] were being fixed [by the Bush administration] around the policy".[4] Astonishingly, this "memo" has been largely ignored by American journalists.[5]

On October 8 of 2002, Senator Bob Graham read a letter to the Senate Intelligence Committee that was sent to him by George Tenet, director of the CIA. The gist of the letter was that Iraq did not pose a serious threat to the U.S. through conventional or chemical/biological weapons. In a press conference on November 7 of the same year, Bush was asked about Tenet's CIA report and reported:

---

3 John B. Judis, *The Folly of Empire: What George W. Bush Could Learn from Theodore Roosevelt and Woodrow Wilson* (New York: Scribner), 176-177.

4 Walter Pincus, "Memo Exposes British Doubts about U.S. Plan for Iraq Invasion", *The Morning Call,* June 12, 2005, A7.

5 See Michael Clark, "Media Ignored Memo: Web Activists Forced U.S. Attention to Secret British Notes", *The Morning Call,* August 28, 2005, D4

> I'm sure he said other sentences.... He sees Saddam Hussein as a threat. I don't know what the context of that quote is. I'm telling you, the guy knows what I know, that he [Hussein] is a problem and we must deal with him.... Well, if we don't do something he might attack us, and he might attack us with a more serious weapon. The man is a threat.... He's a threat because he's dealing with al Qaeda.

Bush, it seems, either knew nothing about the letter and the CIA's report or he was dissembling. The latter is most likely.

In a recent brief press conference in the U.S. with Tony Blair, both leaders were asked to comment on the veracity of the Downing Street Memo. Blair began bluntly, "Well, I can respond to that very easily. No, the facts were not being fixed in any shape or form at all". Bush's replied similarly, though his response, as usual, was anything but smooth-tongued.

> Well, I—you know, I read kind of the characterizations of the memo, particularly when they dropped it out in the middle of his race. I'm not sure who "they dropped it out" is, but—I'm not suggesting that you all dropped it out there. (Yucks.) And somebody said, "Well, you know, we had made up our mind to go to use military force to deal with Saddam". *There's nothing farther from the truth.*
>
> My conversation with the Prime Minister was, "How could we do this peacefully? What could we do?" And this meeting, evidently, that took place in London happened before we even went to the United Nations—or I went to the United Nations. And so it's—look, both us of didn't want to use our military. Nobody wants to commit military into combat. It's the last option. The consequences of committing the military are—are very difficult. The hardest things I do as the President is [*sic*] to try to comfort families who've lost a loved one in combat. It's the last option that the President must have—and it's the last option I know my friend had, as well.
>
> And so we worked hard to see if we could figure out how to do this peacefully, take a—put a united front up to Saddam Hussein, and say, "The world speaks", and he ignored the world. Remember, 1441 passed the Security Council unanimously. He made the decision. And the world is better off without Saddam Hussein in power.
>
> June 7, 2005

Finally, the rhetoric reached its peak with a speech to the American public on June 28 of 2005, where the president, trying to rally public support for continued U.S. presence in Iraq in the midst of growing public dissention, had this to say:

> We fight today because terrorists want to attack our country and kill our citizens, and Iraq is where they are making their stand. So we will fight them there, we will fight them across the world and we will stay in the fight until the fight is won.

Bush would appeal to 9/11 five times in this speech—once again, suggesting a link between 9/11 and Iraq that never existed. House Democratic leader Nancy Pelosi responded, "The president's frequent references to the terrorist attacks of September 11 show the weakness of his arguments. He is willing to exploit the sacred ground of 9/11, knowing that there is no connection between 9/11 and the war in Iraq". Wisconsin senator Russ Feingold noted that the continued military presence in Iraq has made it a breeding ground for terrorists. "The U.S. military presence in Iraq has become a powerful recruiting tool for terrorists, and Iraq is now the premier training ground and networking venue for the next generation of jihadists".

Building a Coalition & Troop Withdrawal

The first debate with John Kerry contains an illuminating exchange between two candidates about the extent to which the U.S. had a coalition of nations when it went into Iraq in Gulf War II. Kerry argued, outside of contributions of Great Britain and Australia, the U.S. was acting unilaterally. Bush countered that America was part of a grand coalition of 30 contributing nations. This statement is factual, but it sidesteps the issue of just what each of these 30 nations is contributing.

> Kerry: The United Nations, Kofi Annan offered help after Baghdad fell. And we never picked him up on that and did what was necessary to transfer authority and to transfer

reconstruction. It was always American-run. Secondly, when we went in, there were three countries: Great Britain, Australia and the United States. That's not a grand coalition. We can do better.

Bush: Well, actually, he forgot Poland. And now there's 30 nations involved [*sic*], standing side by side with our American troops. And I honor their sacrifices. And I don't appreciate it when candidate for president denigrates the contributions of these brave soldiers. You cannot lead the world if you do not honor the contributions of those who are with us. He called them coerced and the bribed. That's not how you bring people together. Our coalition is strong. It will remain strong, so long as I'm the president.

Sept. 30, 2004

Bush boasted that this coalition in Gulf War II was actually larger than that of Gulf War I of 1991, but he could justify this statement only spuriously. Write Ivo Daalder and James Lindsay, "Bush could substantiate that claim only by including such powerhouses as Macedonia, Micronesia, the Marshall Islands, Palau, and Tonga and by ignoring that the Gulf Ward coalition consisted of nations that actually contributed hundreds of thousands of troops and tens of billions of dollars in treasure".[6]

Moreover, it is now well known that Bush, ignoring the advice of certain military advisors, greatly underestimated the number of troops he would need to rebuild Iraq and stave off continual attacks from opposition within Iraq. Having committed up to 200,000 men and women to the country to keep some semblance of order, fight against unrest, and train Iraqis to police their own country, the prospect of long-term stability is proving unrealistic. It is also proving too difficult for the U.S. to handle by itself, which it is essentially doing.

In meantime, Americans are becoming increasingly dissatisfied with the U.S. occupation of Iraq. Constantly badgered by the question "When will the U.S. troops come home?", Bush

6 Ivo H. Daalder and James H. Lindsay, *America Unbound* (Washington, D.C., 2003), 147.

has given and continues to give the same vague answer: When their mission is completed. For example, in a speech in Sioux Falls, South Dakota, on behalf of John Thune's senatorial race, Bush had this to say about troop withdrawal.

> And the other message is this: it doesn't matter how long it takes to secure our freedom; it doesn't matter how long it takes to secure the homeland, we're staying the course. There's no quit in America. *There's not a calendar on my desk that says on such and such a date, bring them home.* That's not how we think. That's not the lesson that John Thune learned from his dad or I learned from my dad or any of us learned from previous generations of people who sacrificed for our freedom.
>
> Apr. 30, 2002

The first debate with Kerry is perhaps the clearest example of Bush's reluctance to say anything concrete about sending troops home.

> Let me first tell you that the best way for Iraq to be safe and secure is for Iraqi citizens to be trained to do the job. And that's what we're doing. We've got 100,000 trained now, 125,000 by the end of this year, 200,000 by the end of next year. That is the best way. We'll never succeed in Iraq if the Iraqi citizens do not want to take matters into their own hands to protect themselves. I believe they want to. Prime Minister Allawi believes they want to. *And so the best indication about when we can bring our troops home—which I really want to do, but I don't want to do so for the sake of bringing them home; I want to do so because we've achieved an objective—is to see the Iraqis perform and to see the Iraqis step up and take responsibility.* And so, the answer to your question is: *When our general is on the ground and Ambassador Negroponte tells me that Iraq is ready to defend herself from these terrorists, that elections will have been held by then, that their stability and that they're on their way to—you know—a nation that's free—that's when.* And I hope it's as soon as possible. But I know putting artificial deadlines won't work.
>
> My opponent at one time said, "Well, get me elected, I'll have them out of there in six months". You can't do that and expect to win the war on terror.
>
> Sept. 30, 2004

More recently, in the *The Washington Post*, Bush used his stock line about troop withdrawal.

> The way I would put it is, *American troops will be leaving as quickly as possible, but they won't be leaving until we have completed our mission.* And part of the mission is to train Iraqis so they can fight the terrorists. And *the sooner the Iraqis are prepared—better prepared, better equipped to fight—the sooner our troops will start coming home.*
>
> Jan. 16, 2005

Finally, in a recent address to the FBI Academy on July 11 of 2005, Bush summed his formula for troop withdrawal succinctly and precisely: "Our plan can be summed up this way: As the Iraqis stand up, we will stand down".

Overall, Bush's lack of verbal clarity sends a demoralizing message to young men and women, who risk their lives each day to complete a mission that is, at best, vaguely articulated. The unambiguous signal this sends to the troops is that their lives are less important than his plans in Iraq—whatever these may be.

Chapter 2
The Bush Doctrine

"The executioner's argument [about whether you could cut off the Chesire-Cat's head] was, that you couldn't cut off a head unless there was a body to cut it off from: that he had never had to do such a thing before, and he wasn't going to begin at his *time of life.*

"The King's argument was that anything that had a head could be beheaded, and that you weren't talking nonsense.

"The Queen's argument was that, if something wasn't done about it in less than no time, she'd have everybody executed, all round".

Liberalism

In social and political philosophy, *liberalism* is a common term that means different things to different advocates. In general, it concerns individuals' rights in governments that are considered open and free. Libertarian liberals emphasize individual rights in a free-market economy, where the state exercises its power only to maintain maximum freedom. Communitarian liberals argue that there is greater need of social structure and constraints to allow freedom to flourish. Egalitarian liberals focus on equality for all. One such way of ensuring equality is to focus on human welfare.

What is Bush's view of liberalism? Some of the president's most moving speeches focus on liberalism, which for him is a tendentious admixture of freedom, respect for human dignity, human rights, equality, and universal values, among other things.

Shortly after 9/11, Bush rationalized the attack on America in the following manner:

> On the Korean War Memorial in Washington are these words, "Freedom is not free". Our commitment to freedom has always made us a target of tyranny and intolerance. *Anyone who sets out to destroy freedom must eventually attack America,* because *we're freedom's home.* And we must always be freedom's home and freedom's defender. We must never flinch in the face of adversity, and we won't.
>
> "Lessons of Liberty", Oct. 30, 2001

The U.S. was attacked not for its intrusion in Middle-East affairs, but rather because America is "freedom's home".

Bush articulated his notion of American liberalism best in a speech delivered to the graduating class at West Point on June 1 of 2002. The address is one of the most stirring of all speeches that the president has ever given. Unfortunately, given his track record for mendacity, dissembling, and duplicity, it is also one of the most hypocritical speeches he has ever given.

> The 20th century ended with a single surviving model of human progress, based on non-negotiable demands of human dignity, the rule of law, limits on the power of the state, respect for women and private property and free speech and equal justice and religious tolerance. America cannot impose this vision—yet we can support and reward governments that make the right choices for their own people. In our development aid, in our diplomatic efforts, in our international broadcasting, and in our educational assistance, the United States will promote moderation and tolerance and human rights. And we will defend the peace that makes all progress possible.
>
> When it comes to the common rights and needs of men and women, there is no clash of civilizations. The requirements of freedom apply fully to Africa and Latin America and the entire Islamic world. The peo-

> ples of the Islamic nations want and deserve the same freedoms and opportunities as people in every nation. And their governments should listen to their hopes.
>
> A truly strong nation will permit legal avenues of dissent for all groups that pursue their aspirations without violence. An advancing nation will pursue economic reform, to unleash the great entrepreneurial energy of its people. A thriving nation will respect the rights of women, because no society can prosper while denying opportunity to half its citizens. Mothers and fathers and children across the Islamic world, and all the world [*sic*], share the same fears and aspirations. In poverty, they struggle. In tyranny, they suffer. And as we saw in Afghanistan, in liberation, they celebrate.

Bush baldly asserts here "America cannot impose this vision" of dignity, respect, toleration, and justice. Yet this is just what it as done with the invasion of Iraq.

In a press conference on January 26 of 2005, Bush emphasized that liberalism is about recognition of universal values, which are essentially democratic values.

> And I believe this country is best when it heads toward an ideal world. We are at our best. And in doing so, we're reflecting universal values and universal ideas that honor each man and woman, that recognize human rights and human dignity depends upon human liberty.... But we expect nations to adopt the values inherent in a democracy, which is [*sic*] human rights and human dignity, that every person matters and every person ought to have a voice.
>
> Jan. 26, 2005

At a roundtable discussion in Germany, Bush emphasized some new insights he gained from a recently read book, *The Case for Democracy.* Bush spoke with the giddy glee of a college freshman whose in-class comments are positively reinforced by a professor.

> First of all, Sharansky's book confirmed how I was raised and what I believe, and it's essentially this: that deep in everybody's soul—everybody's soul—is this deep desire to be free. That's what I believe. No matter where you're raised, no matter your religion, people want to be free; and that a foreign policy, particularly from a nation that is free,

> ought to be based upon that thought. You know, you can't discriminate. Freedom is not a discriminatory thought, at least in the White House—in other words, if you say, certain people should be free, but others shouldn't free [*sic*]. It's a universal thought, as far as I'm concerned. And therefore, our foreign policy is based upon this notion that the world is a better place when people are able to realize that which is embedded in their soul, *because in that book, also, he talks about the idea that free societies are peaceful societies—democratic societies don't attack each other.* And Europe is a classic example of countries which have embraced values based upon democracy, and is peaceful.
>
> Feb. 23, 2005

Two things are worth noting here. First, Bush's use of the words "therefore" and "because" in the sixth sentence indicate clearly that he considers the author himself to be sufficient justification for the conclusion: "The world is a better place when people are free". I'm not contesting the claim, only the manner in which it is considered to be true: authority of authorship is taken to be sufficient evidence for it. Second, "democratic societies don't attack each other" may be true, though it is scarcely obviously true, but Bush's preemptive actions in Iraq show plainly that "democratic" and "peace-loving" societies do attack those that are not democratic.

In addition, there's the president's hard-nosed inaugural address of January 20 of 2005. Its appeal to universal values is grounded in the "Maker of Heaven and Earth".

> From the day of our Founding, *we have proclaimed* that every man and woman on this earth has rights, and dignity, and matchless value, because they bear the image of the Maker of Heaven and Earth. Across the generations *we have proclaimed the imperative* of self-government, because no one is fit to be a master, and no one deserves to be a slave. Advancing these ideals is the mission that created our Nation. It is the honorable achievement of our fathers. Now it is the urgent *requirement* of our nation's security, and the calling of our time. So, it is the policy of the United States to seek and support the growth of democratic movements and institutions in every nation and culture, with the ultimate goal of ending tyranny in our world....
>
> America's belief in human dignity will guide our policies, yet *rights*

> *must be more than the grudging concessions of dictators*; they are secured by free dissent and the participation of the governed. In the long run, there is no justice without freedom, and there can be no human rights without human liberty.

Finally, liberalism for Bush entails "expanding freedom at home" and "expanding liberty abroad".

> By expanding freedom at home, we will provide our citizens, all our citizens, the path of greater opportunity and more control over their own lives. And by expanding liberty abroad, we'll provide our citizens with security—the security they need to build a prosperous and peaceful future for their children.
>
> Mar. 15, 2005

Preemption

It may be obvious by now that Bush's notion of liberalism, based on universally recognizable values set in place by God, authorizes him to take preemptive measures, if needed, to ensure America's safety and to promote global freedom. This stands in sharp contrast to the vision of American foreign policy he had prior to becoming president.

In his first debate with Al Gore, moderator Jim Lehrer asked, "How would you go about as president deciding when it was in the national interest to use U.S. force, generally?" Bush gave four conditions—presumably, each being necessary and all, taken together, being jointly sufficient for going to war. The reply was essentially the "Powell Doctrine".

> Well, if its in our vital national interest, and that means whether our territory is threatened or people could be harmed, whether or not the alliances are—our defense alliances are threatened, whether or not our friends in the Middle East are threatened. That would be a time to seriously consider the use of force. *Secondly*, whether or not the mission was clear. Whether or not it was a clear understanding as to what the mission would be. *Thirdly*, whether or not we were prepared and trained

> to win. Whether or not our forces were of high morale and high standing and well-equipped. And *finally*, whether or not there was an exit strategy. I would take the use of force very seriously. I would be guarded in my approach.
>
> I don't think we can be all things to all people in the world. I think we've got to be very careful when we commit our troops. The vice president and I have a disagreement about the use of troops. *He believes in nation building. I would be very careful about using our troops as nation builders. I believe the role of the military is to fight and win war and therefore prevent war from happening in the first place* [*sic*]. So I would take my responsibility seriously.
>
> Oct. 3, 2000

Here again two points are worth making. First, it is noteworthy that perhaps none of these conditions were met in the invasion of Iraq. Second, there is the completely asinine claim that the role of the military is to prevent war from happening "in the first place" by going to war and winning that war. The notion of using war to prevent war is a sufficiently disquieting thought in itself, if this is what Bush really meant to say.

In the second debate with Gore, Bush reiterated his conservatism and guardedness on the topic of war.

> So I'm not exactly sure where the vice president is coming from, but I think *one way for us to end up being viewed as the ugly American is for us to go around the world saying, "We do it this way, so should you."* Now, we trust freedom. We know freedom is a powerful, powerful, powerful force, much bigger than the United States of America, as we saw recently in the Balkans. But maybe I misunderstand where you're coming from, Mr. Vice President, but I think *the United States must be humble and must be proud and confident of our values, but humble in how we treat nations that are figuring out how to chart their own course.*
>
> Oct. 11, 2000

After becoming president, the administration's position dramatically changed after 9/11. In his first debate with John Kerry, Bush argued for an aggressive policy to ensure America's security, as the risks of a defensive, conservative posture were too great.

[T]he best way to protect this homeland is to stay on the offense. You know, we have to be right 100 percent of the time. And the enemy only has to be right once to hurt us. There's a lot of good people *[sic]* working hard. And by the way, we've also changed the culture of the FBI to have counterterrorism as its number one priority. We're communicating better. We're going to reform our intelligence services to make sure that we get the best intelligence possible. The Patriot Act is vital—is vital that the Congress renew the Patriot Act which enables our law enforcement to disrupt terror cells. But again, I repeat to my fellow citizens, *the best way to protection is to stay on the offense.*

Sept. 30, 2004

Again, in his address to graduates at West Point, Bush reiterates his innovative strike-first-and-then-ask-questions-later policy. Deterrence may have been a viable Cold-War strategy, but it cannot work against terrorism.

For much of the last century, America's defense relied on the Cold War doctrines of deterrence and containment. In some cases, those strategies still apply. But new threats also require new thinking. Deterrence—the promise of massive retaliation against nations—means nothing against shadowy terrorist networks with no nation or citizens to defend. Containment is not possible when unbalanced dictators with weapons of mass destruction can deliver those weapons on missiles or secretly provide them to terrorist allies....

[T]he war on terror will not be won on the defensive. We must take the battle to the enemy, disrupt his plans, and confront the worst threats before they emerge. *In the world we have entered, the only path to safety is the path of action. And this nation will act....*

[O]ur security will require all Americans to be forward-looking and resolute, to be ready for preemptive action when necessary to defend our liberty and to defend our lives.

June 1, 2002

At a press conference on April 28 of 2005, Bush repeated the theme of staying on the offensive side in the war against terrorism.

Reporter: Mr. President, your State Department has reported that terrorist attacks around the world are at an all-time high. If

	we're winning the war on terrorism, as you say, how do you explain that more people are dying in terrorist attacks on your watch than ever before?
Bush:	Well, we've made the decision *to defeat the terrorists abroad so we don't have to face them here at home*. And when you engage the terrorists abroad, it causes activity and action. And we're relentless. We, the—America and our coalition partners—we understand the stakes, and they're very high because there are people still out there that would like to do harm to the American people. *But our strategy is to stay on the offense, is to keep the pressure on these people, is to cut off their money and to share intelligence and to find them where they hide.* And we are making good progress. The al Qaeda network that attacked the United States has been severely diminished. We are slowly but surely dismantling that organization. *In the long run, Terry—like I said earlier—the way to defeat terror, though, is to spread freedom and democracy.* It's really the only way in the long-term. In the short-term, we'll use our troops and assets and agents to find these people and to protect America. But in the long-term, we must defeat the hopelessness that allows them to recruit by spreading freedom and democracy. But we're making progress.
Reporter:	So in the near-term you think there will be more attacks and more people dying?
Bush:	I'm not going to predict that. In the near-term I can only tell you one thing: *we will stay on the offense; we'll be relentless;* we'll be smart about how we go after the terrorists; we'll use our friends and allies to go after the terrorists; we will find them where they hide and bring them to justice.

Finally, I give some additional key passages on preemption to illustrate the radical shift in Bush's position on the use of American forces abroad.

> Some who call themselves "realists" question whether the spread of democracy in the Middle East should be any concern of ours. But the realists in this case have lost contact with a fundamental reality. America has always been less secure when freedom is in retreat. *America is always more secure when freedom is on the march.*
>
> U.S. Air Force Academy, June 2, 2004

We deal with threats before they fully materialize. What that means is that in the old days you could see a threat, and you may deal with it or you may not deal with it, but you never thought a threat would come to harm us. Those days are gone.

Interview with Rush Limbaugh, Aug. 31, 2004

The United States has no right, no desire, and no intention to impose our form of government on anyone else. That is one of the main differences between us and our enemies. They seek to impose and expand an empire of oppression, in which a tiny group of brutal, self-appointed rulers control every aspect of every life. *Our aim is to build and preserve a community of free and independent nations, with governments that answer to their citizens, and reflect their own cultures.* And because democracies respect their own people and their neighbors, the advance of freedom will lead to peace.

State of the Union Address, Feb. 2, 2005

One of my—I've said this before to you, I'm going to say it again—one of my concerns after September the 11th is the farther away we got from September the 11th, the more relaxed we would all become and assume that there wasn't an enemy out there ready to hit us. And I just can't let the American people—I'm not going to let them down by assuming that the enemy is not going to hit us again. We're going to do everything we can to protect us. And we've got guidelines. We've got law. But you bet...we're going to find people before they harm us.

Apr. 28, 2005

Unilateralism

Bush has made it clear on several occasions that he is first and foremost concerned about what's in America's best interest. One instance is his refusal to join the International Criminal Court in The Hague, which shows that he doesn't want the U.S. to be held accountable to the same global standards of right and wrong to which others nations are willing to be held.

And that is, I wouldn't join the International Criminal Court. It's a body based in The Hague where unaccountable judges and prosecutors can pull our troops or diplomats up for trial. And I wouldn't join it. And I

> understand that in certain capitals around the world that that wasn't a popular move. But it's the right move not to join a foreign court that could—where our people could be prosecuted. My opponent is for joining the International Criminal Court. I just think trying to be popular, kind of, in the global sense, if it's not in our best interest makes no sense. I'm interested in working with our nations and do a lot of it. But I'm not going to make decisions that I think are wrong for America.
>
> Bush/Kerry I, Sept. 30, 2004

Another example is his insistence that the Kyoto treaty, making nations accountable for their contribution to global pollution, is wrong for America.

> Well, had we joined the Kyoto treaty, which I guess he's referring to, it would have cost America a lot of jobs. It's one of these deals where, in order to be popular in the halls of Europe, you sign a treaty. But I thought it would cost a lot—I think there's a better way to do it.
>
> Bush/Kerry II, Oct. 8, 2004

This second instance especially shows clearly that Bush's thinking on political and moral issues is inescapably short-term. He often seems incapable of seeing what the cost of a decision might be many years later. Tightening up pollution standards would certainly cost the U.S. jobs in the short-term, but what of the cost of inaction on the issue of pollution in the long-term?

One other such issue that is linked with what's in America's best interest is a third element of the Bush Doctrine—unilateralism. Again, returning to the second debate with Kerry, Bush makes it clear that America has no need of passing a "global test", when it comes to American interests.

> Let me—I'm not exactly sure what you mean, "passes the global test"—you take preemptive action if you pass a global test. My attitude is you take preemptive action in order to protect the American people, that you act in order to make this country secure.
>
> Sept. 30, 2004

Bush's staff was quick to pick up on the global-test rhetoric. In his second debate with Kerry, Bush stated:

> You remember the last debate? My opponent said that America must pass a global test before we used force to protect ourselves. That's the kind of mindset that says sanctions were working. That's the kind of mindset that said, "Let's keep it at the United Nations and hope things go well".
>
> Oct. 8, 2004

In an address to Central African Leaders in New York on September 13 of 2002, Bush was explicit that the U.S. ought not to consider what the United Nations has to say, when it comes to what's in the best interest of America.

> Reporter: Mr. President, thank you. Are you concerned that Democrats in Congress don't want a vote there until after U.N. action? And secondly, have you spoken with President Putin since your speech yesterday?
>
> Bush: I have not spoken to President Putin since my speech. I did speak to his Foreign Minister, as did Colin Powell. I'll speak to President Putin, I'm confident, soon. I'll have—I think we've got a scheduled phone call, actually. And the first part of the question was, Democrats waiting for the U.N. to act? I can't imagine an elected United States—elected member of the United States Senate or House of Representatives saying, "I think I'm going to wait for the United Nations to make a decision". It seems like to me that if you're representing the United States, you ought to be making a decision on what's best for the United States. If I were running for office [*sic*], I'm not sure how I'd explain to the American people—say, "Vote for me, and, oh, by the way, on a matter of national security, I think I'm going to wait for somebody else to act". And so I—we'll see. My answer to the Congress is, they need to debate this issue and consult with us, and get the issue done as quickly as possible. It's in our national interests that we do so. I don't imagine Saddam Hussein sitting around, saying, "Gosh, I think I'm going to wait for some resolution". He's a threat that we must deal with as quickly as possible.
>
> Sept. 13, 2002

Finally, the president's State of the Union Address in 2004 emphasized flatly that the U.S. is not afraid to go it alone, as it were, when it comes to its own security.

> From the beginning, America has sought international support for our operations in Afghanistan and Iraq, and we have gained much support. There is a difference, however, between leading a coalition of many nations, and submitting to the objections of a few. *America will never seek a permission slip to defend the security of our country.*

Officium Paci

The final component of the Bush Doctrine is what I call "*Officium Paci*" (lit., "a duty for peace). In places, Bush almost in ministerial fashion talks of America's duty to promote peace globally. This is perhaps a divinely inspired calling—as the president often hints it is—to spread freedom and democracy to the rest of the world by Americanizing the globe.

I begin with his speech to the West Point graduating class on June 1 of 2002, where Bush talks of defending, preserving, and extending a "just peace".

> This war will take many turns we cannot predict. Yet I am certain of this: Wherever we carry it, the American flag will stand not only for our power, but for freedom. *Our nation's cause has always been larger than our nation's defense. We fight, as we always fight, for a just peace—a peace that favors human liberty. We will defend the peace* against threats from terrorists and tyrants. *We will preserve the peace* by building good relations among the great powers. And *we will extend the peace* by encouraging free and open societies on every continent.
>
> Building this just peace is America's opportunity, and America's duty. From this day forward, it is your challenge, as well, and we will meet this challenge together. You will wear the uniform of a great and unique country. America has no empire to extend or utopia to establish. We wish for others only what we wish for ourselves—safety from violence, the rewards of liberty, and the hope for a better life....
>
> America has a greater objective than controlling threats and containing resentment. We will work for a just and peaceful world beyond the war on terror.

The State of the Union Address of 2003 is just one of numerous places where Bush calls America's liberty "God's gift to humanity".

> We seek peace. We strive for peace. And sometimes peace must be defended. A future, lived at the mercy of terrible threats, is no peace at all. *If war is forced upon us,* we will fight in a just cause and by just means—sparing, in every way we can, the innocent. And *if war is forced upon us,* we will fight with the full force and might of the United States military—and we will prevail….
>
> Americans are a free people, who know that freedom is the right of every person and the future of every nation. *The liberty we prize is not America's gift to the world, it is God's gift to humanity.*

This duty to spread peace, of course, does not rule out preemptive military measures, if deemed required. Bush's hard-hitting inaugural address on January 20 of 2005 made this at least implicitly clear.

> We are led, by events and common sense, to one conclusion: The survival of liberty in our land increasingly depends on the success of liberty in other lands. The best hope for peace in our world is the expansion of freedom in all the world.

In an interview with Brit Hume, Bush unabashedly labeled his belief that military measures must be taken to promote global peace "active foreign policy".

> But there is a longer-term issue as well, and that is, how do you change attitudes? What is necessary to defeat that sentiment that causes people to be suiciders and just kill innocent people for the sake of religion or a fake religion? And my judgment on that is the best way to do it is to spread freedom. I equate freedom and peace. And *I believe America, given its position in the world, must use our power to promote freedom.* And that's precisely what this administration is doing…. And many Americans also understand what I know to be true: *free societies are peaceful societies.* And that's why I will continue to promote what I would call an *"active foreign policy".*
>
> Sept. 22, 2003

I end, fittingly enough, with a final quote from Bush's West Point speech.

> Speaking here to the class of 1942—six months after Pearl Harbor—General Marshall said, "We're determined that before the sun sets on this terrible struggle, our flag will be recognized throughout the world as a symbol of freedom on the one hand, and of *overwhelming power* on the other".

Chapter 3
Political Miscellanea

"'Well, in our country', said Alice, still panting a little, 'you'd generally get to somewhere else—if you ran very fast for a long time, as we've been doing'.

"'A slow sort of country!' said the Queen. 'Now, here *you see, it takes all the running* you *can do, to keep in the same place. If you want to get somewhere else, you must run at least twice as fast as that!'"*

Bush on America

The preceding chapter should give readers a good sense of the president's political agenda for the U.S. as it relates to the rest of the world. Stated simply, it amounts to attempting to globalize his unique vision of America's greatness.

Just what makes America so great? Bush's Inaugural Address in January 20 of 2005, with substantial chunks given below, tells us plainly—freedom. I quote at length.

> There is only one force of history that can break the reign of hatred and resentment, and expose the pretensions of tyrants, and reward the hopes of the decent and tolerant, and that is the force of human *freedom.*
>
> We are led, by events and common sense, to one conclusion: The

survival of *liberty* in our land increasingly depends on the success of *liberty* in other lands. The best hope for peace in our world is the expansion of *freedom* on all the world….

Freedom, by its nature, must be chosen, and defended by citizens, and sustained by the rule of law and the protection of minorities….

America's belief in human dignity will guide our policies, yet rights must be more than the grudging concessions of dictators; they are secured by *free* dissent and the participation of the governed. In the long run, there is no justice without *freedom*, and there can be no human rights without human liberty….

By our efforts, we have lit a fire as well—a fire in the minds of men. It warms those who feel its power, it burns those who fight its progress, and one day this untamed fire of freedom will reach the darkest corners of our world….

Make the choice to serve in a cause larger than your wants, larger than yourself—and in your days you will add not just to the wealth of our country, but to its character. America has need of idealism and courage, because we have essential work at home—the unfinished work of American *freedom*. In a world moving toward *liberty*, we are determined to show the meaning and promise of *liberty*….

By making every citizen an agent of his or her own destiny, we will give our fellow Americans greater *freedom* from want and fear, and make our society more prosperous and just and equal. In America's ideal of *freedom*, the public interest depends on private character—on integrity, and tolerance toward others, and the rule of conscience in our own lives. Self-government relies, in the end, on the governing of the self….

In America's ideal of *freedom*, the exercise of rights is ennobled by service, and mercy, and a heart for the weak. *Liberty* for all does not mean independence from one another. Our nation relies on men and women who look after a neighbor and surround the lost with love. Americans, at our best, value the life we see in one another, and must always remember that even the unwanted have worth….

These questions that judge us also unite us, because Americans of every party and background, Americans by choice and by birth, are bound to one another in the cause of *freedom*….

We go forward with complete confidence in the eventual triumph of *freedom*. Not because history runs on the wheels of inevitability; it is human choices that move events. Not because we consider ourselves a chosen nation; God moves and chooses as He wills. We have confidence because *freedom* is the permanent hope of mankind, the hunger in dark places, the longing of the soul. When our Founders declared a new order of the ages; when soldiers died in wave upon wave for a union based on

> *liberty*; when citizens marched in peaceful outrage under the banner "*Freedom* Now"—they were acting on an ancient hope that is meant to be fulfilled. History has an ebb and flow of justice, but history also has a visible direction, set by *liberty* and the Author of *Liberty*.
>
> When the Declaration of Independence was first read in public and the Liberty Bell was sounded in celebration, a witness said, "It rang as if it meant something". In our time it means something still. America, in this young century, proclaims *liberty* throughout all the world, and to all the inhabitants thereof. Renewed in our strength—tested, but not weary—we are ready for the greatest achievements in the history of *freedom*.

This address was a triumph of propaganda over truth. The hypocrisy in the propaganda was evident from the start. In the relatively short speech, the words "free" or "freedom" appear 34 times; the word "liberty", 16 times. Moreover, the meaning of these terms varies wildly with usage. One is reminded of the inconsistencies of Bush's *officium paci*.

What, other than freedom, makes American so great? Addressing members of the Islamic Center in Washington, DC, days after 9/11, Bush mentioned America's values.

> This is a great country. It's a great country because we share the same values of respect and dignity and human worth. And it is my honor to be meeting with leaders who feel just the same way I do. They're outraged, they're sad. They love America just as much as I do.
>
> Sept. 17, 2001

And, of course, let no one forget what is possibly the greatest value—America's ability to love—which presumably far outstrips that of other countries.

> But the true strength of America is found in the hearts and souls of people like Travis, people who are willing to love their neighbor, just like they would like to love themselves.
>
> Springfield, MO, Feb. 9, 2004

We also learn that America is so virtuous that even its mountains smack of values.

> There's also a grand vision embodied in these mountains [i.e., the Rockies]. And the vision is that we can teach our children right from wrong. And we can teach them good, sound values, so that when they get older they'll make the right choices in life.
>
> Aug. 14, 2001

To teach children right from wrong, one need only spend a weekend camping in the Rockies. This by itself may explain why Bush has not fully funded his pet educational project, No Child Left Behind.

Welcoming immigrants on Ellis Island to America, Bush said the following about this great country to those listening and even those not listening.

> It's my honor to speak to you as the leader of your country. And the great thing about America is you don't have to listen unless you want to.
>
> July 10, 2001

Finally, being an American means taking a clear stand on issues. As Bush himself said in Davenport, Iowa, on August 5 of 2004, "We stand for things".

Bush on Terrorism

The saying "One person's freedom fighter is another person's terrorist" suggests that terrorism is a greatly misunderstood and misdiagnosed phenomenon. The misunderstanding and misdiagnosis reflect, in part, the existing definitional confusion in the scholarship on terrorism.

Minimally *terrorism* is a type of political violence whose aim is to incite terror. Yet this is a definition that is too thin. Along these lines, the U.S.'s bombings of Dresden, Nagasaki, and Hiroshima were terrorist activities. So, too are all acts of war.

Yet it seems that the types of activities of the Islamic organizations that bombed the marine barracks in Beirut in 1983, rammed an explosives-filled boat into the USS Cole in 2000, and were responsible for the atrocities of 9/11 seem to be different. For instance, Al Qaeda, behind the events of 9/11, was founded in 1989 by Osama bin Laden—a crusader for no nation, but instead for Arabic culture—whose aims have been to drive the United States and Israel out of the Middle East and to punish those Arab regimes that are dependent on the U.S. or Israel. Islamic organizations like al Qaeda are, as Bill Clinton said, not state-sponsored groups, but "enemies of the nation-state".[1] And so, by "terrorism" let us understand a type of political violence to persons or property by non-state agents for the purpose of reaching political goals through inciting fear. Given this, the acts of terrorists differ mostly from acts of war in that these acts are committed by agents not representing any one state or nation.

Bush's use of the term "terrorist" generally conforms to this definition. Consider an address shortly after 9/11:

> The terrorists practice a fringe form of Islamic extremism that has been rejected by Muslim scholars and the vast majority of Muslim clerics—a fringe movement that perverts the peaceful teachings of Islam. The terrorists' directive commands them to kill Christians and Jews, to kill all Americans, and make no distinction among military and civilians, including women and children.
>
> This group and its leader—a person named Osama bin Laden—are linked to many other organizations in different countries, including the Egyptian Islamic Jihad and the Islamic Movement of Uzbekistan. There are thousands of these terrorists in more than 60 countries. They are recruited from their own nations and neighborhoods and brought to camps in places like Afghanistan, where they are trained in the tactics of terror. They are sent back to their homes or sent to hide in countries around the world to plot evil and destruction....

---

[1] John Judis, *The Folly of Empire*, 163.

> These terrorists kill not merely to end lives, but to disrupt and end a way of life. With every atrocity, they hope that America grows fearful, retreating from the world and forsaking our friends. They stand against us, because we stand in their way.
>
> Sept. 20, 2001

On January 29 of 2002, Bush explicitly stated what the U.S.'s two objectives were in hunting down terrorists.

> Our nation will continue to be steadfast and patient and persistent in the pursuit of two great objectives. First, we will shut down terrorist camps, disrupt terrorist plans, and bring terrorists to justice. And, second, we must prevent the terrorists and regimes who seek chemical, biological or nuclear weapons from threatening the United States and the world.

Again, consider further articulations of his Identity-of-Bedfellows Principle—the former, focusing on guilt, the latter, on desert:

> I also want to make it clear that the doctrine I laid out to the United States Congress is a doctrine this nation will enforce. It says clearly that if you harbor a terrorist, if you feed a terrorist, if you provide sanctuary to a terrorist, if you fund a terrorist, you are just as guilty as the terrorist that inflicted the harm on the American people.
>
> "Lessons of Liberty", Oct. 30, 2001

> We said, "If you harbor a terrorist, you're just like the terrorist, we're going to treat you just like the terrorist". And we upheld that doctrine by removing the Taliban.
>
> July 1, 2002

Yet, not surprisingly, Bush's conception of "terrorism" is a politicized conception that has taken on his *officium paci* mission. In an address to the U.S. Air Force Academy in 2004, Bush compared terrorist to totalitarians, who attempt to crush liberty globally and supplant it with the tyranny of "colorless conformity". It seems clear that he had the old Soviet Union in mind here.

> Like the murderous ideologies of the 20th century, the ideology of terrorism reaches across boarders, and seeks recruits in every country. So we're fighting these enemies wherever they hide across the earth. *Like other totalitarian movements, the terrorists seek to impose a grim vision in which dissent is crushed, and every man and woman must think and live in colorless conformity.* So *to the oppressed peoples everywhere, we are offering the great alternative of human liberty.* Like enemies of the past, the terrorists underestimate the strength of free peoples. *The terrorists believe that free societies are essentially corrupt and decadent,* and with a few hard blows will collapse in weakness and in panic. The enemy has learned that America is strong and determined, because of the steady resolve of our citizens, and because of the skill and strength of the Army, Navy, Marines, Coast Guard and the United States Air Force….
>
> June 2, 2004

In the same address, Bush attempted to deals with a common objection to his "active foreign policy": Hunting out terrorists is like stirring up a hornet's nest.

> *Some say that by fighting the terrorists abroad since September the 11th, we only stir up a hornet's nest.* But the terrorists who struck that day were stirred up already. If America were not fighting terrorists in Iraq, and Afghanistan, and elsewhere, *what would these thousands of killers do, suddenly begin leading productive lives of service and charity? Would the terrorists who beheaded an American on camera just be quiet, peaceful citizens if America had not liberated Iraq?* We are dealing here with killers who have made the death of Americans the calling of their lives. And America has made a decision about these terrorists: *Instead of waiting for them to strike again in our midst, we will take this fight to the enemy.*

Here and everywhere that he confronts the issue of terrorism, Bush makes two fundamental mistakes. First, he fails to recognize, perhaps for propagandist reasons, the psychological motivation behind the strikes of 9/11. They were done with full anticipation of retaliation. In fact, al Qaeda was banking on retaliation to gain further support for their jihad. As such, a blind let's-take-the-war-to-them approach to eradicating terrorism may ultimately do more to fan, than put out, the flame. Second, by using the rhetoric of good versus evil, freedom versus oppression, and order versus chaos, he fails to address the explicit reasons why al Qaeda is targeting America: They want Islamic culture to be Islamic, not American. They want the U.S. out of the Middle East.

In a press conference on May 31 of 2005, Bush explains that the terrorists kill as they do because they understand, just as clearly as Bush does, the "benefits" of democracy. The reasoning is absurd.

> These are incredibly hopeful times—and very difficult times. And the problem is, is that I not only see the benefits of democracy, but *so do the terrorists.* And that's why they want to blow people up, indiscriminately kill, in order to shake the will of the Iraqis, or perhaps create a civil war, or to get us to withdraw early. That's what they're trying to do, because they fear democracy. *They understand what I just—they understand what I understand. There's kind of a meeting of minds on that.* And that's why the American people are seeing violent actions on their TV screens, because these people want to—the killers want us to get out. They want us to—they want the Iraqis to quit. They understand what a democracy can mean to their backward way of thinking.

If this wasn't plain enough, Bush articulated precisely on how September 11 changed things globally on June 29 of 2005.

> And the context of September the 11th was this. We came—we learned firsthand the nature of the war on terror on September the 11th, so when the war first came here is what I say. The last time I went to Europe I said something, which is true, I said, and many in Europe viewed September the 11th as a tragic moment, but a moment. I viewed it—view September the 11th as an attack as a result of a larger war that changed how I view the world, as did—and how many other Americans view the world. It was one of these moments in history that changed outlook.

Finally, there is Bush's single-minded plan for dealing with the terrorists:

> We do know that terrorists murder in the name of a totalitarian ideology that hates freedom, rejects tolerance and despises all dissent. Their aim—the aim of the terrorists is to remake the Middle East in their own grim image of tyranny and oppression by toppling governments, by exporting terror, by forcing free nations to retreat and withdraw.
>
> FBI Academy, July 11, 2005

Bush on Religion

From the start Bush has been a controversial figure, in part, because of his dogged refusal to keep issues of politics and religion separate. In a column for the *Los Angeles Times* on January 24 of 2001, Alan Dershowitz writes:

> The very first act of the new Bush administration was to have a Protestant Evangelist minister officially dedicate the inauguration to Jesus Christ, whom he declared to be "our savior." Invoking "the Father, the Son, the Lord Jesus Christ" and "the Holy Spirit," Billy Graham's son, the man selected by President George W. Bush to bless his presidency, excluded the tens of millions of Americans who are Muslims, Jews, Buddhists, Shintoists, Unitarians, agnostics, and atheists from his blessing by his particularistic and parochial language.
>
> The plain message conveyed by the new administration is that George W. Bush's America is a Christian nation and that non-Christians are welcome into the tent so long as they agree to accept their status as a tolerated minority rather than as fully equal citizens. In effect, Bush is saying: "This is our home, and in our home we pray to Jesus as our savior. If you want to be a guest in our home, you must accept the way we pray."[2]

Bush scored points with Evangelicals at the GOP debate in Iowa on December 13 of 1999 when he called "Christ" his favorite political philosopher. He refers to this incident in an interview with Beliefnet.com in 2000.

---

2 Alan M. Dershowitz, "Bush Starts Off by Defying the Constitution", *Los Angeles Times,* January 24, 2001.

> I mean, during a debate I was asked about [my favorite political] philosopher. I answered, "Christ". They said, "Why?" I said, "Because it changed my heart". And the guy in front of him on TV said, "Well explain what that means". Well that's kind of hard to do in sound-bite fashion—when somebody becomes a religious person—why that causes somebody to be less likely to use drugs. It's very difficult, at least it is for me, to explain it.

Was Bush's answer sincere or was it given merely to procure votes? He can be absolved of fraud, if the answer was sincere, but not of ignorance. Christ was certainly not much of a political philosopher.

In addition, consider this exchange between Bush and Helen Thomas, a veteran journalist held in considerable esteem at the White House, on the issue of the inconsistency of a secular U.S. official supporting faith-based initiatives.

Reporter:	Mr. President, why do you refuse to respect the wall between the church and state? And you know that the mixing of religion and government for centuries has led to slaughter. I mean, the very fact that our country has stood in good stead by having the separation—why do you break it down?
Bush:	Helen, I strongly respect the separation of church and state—
Reporter:	Well, you wouldn't have a religious office in the White House, if you did.
Bush:	I didn't get to finish my answer, in all due respect. I believe that so long as there's a secular alternative available, we ought to allow individuals who are helping to be able to choose a program that may be run by a faith-based program—or will be run by a faith-based program. I understand full well that some of the most compassionate missions of help and aid come out of faith-based programs. And I strongly support the faith-based initiative that we're proposing, because *I don't believe it violates the line between the separation of church and state*, and *I believe it's going to make America a better place.*
Reporter:	Well, you are a secular official—
Bush:	I agree. I am a secular official.
Reporter:	—and not a missionary.

Feb. 22, 2001

The conversation ended abruptly with Bush turning to another reporter to field a different question.

Bush spoke in great detail about the role of religion and prayer in his life in the third debate with John Kerry:

> First, my faith plays a lot—a big part in my life. …I pray a lot. And I do. And my faith is a very—it's very personal. I pray for strength. I pray for wisdom. I pray for our troops in harm's way. I pray for my family. I pray for my little girls. But I'm mindful in a free society that people can worship if they want to or not. You're equally an American if you choose to worship an almighty and if you choose not to. If you're a Christian, Jew or Muslim, you're equally an American. That's the great thing about America, is the right to worship the way you see fit. Prayer and religion sustain me. I receive calmness in the storms of the presidency. I love the fact that people pray for me and my family all around the country. Somebody asked me one time, "Well, how do you know?" I said, "I just feel it".
>
> Religion is an important part. I never want to impose my religion on anybody else. But when I make decisions, I stand on principle, and the principles are derived from who I am. I believe we ought to love our neighbor like we love ourself [*sic*] *manifested in public policy through the faith-based initiative where we've unleashed the armies of compassion to help heal people who hurt.* I believe that *God wants everybody to be free.* That's what I believe. And that's been part of my foreign policy. *In Afghanistan,* I believe that *the freedom there is a gift from the Almighty.* And I can't tell you how encouraged I am to see freedom on the march. And so my principles that I make decisions on are a part of me, and religion is a part of me.
>
> Oct. 13, 2004

Afghanistan is, of course, still the world's leading opium-producing country and as of this writing the situation in Afghanistan is still dreadfully chaotic. The hypocrisy here is perhaps criminal.

Bush has also come under fire early in his second term for nominating a good number of judges that are ultra-conservatives. In this exchange with a reporter, Bush is asked first about his discontent with political opposition to his recent nominations and secondly about the role that faith is increasingly playing in political debates. As is his wont, he sidesteps the first question—though in no artful manner—and addresses a slightly different version of the second question.

Bush:	The role of religion in our society? I view religion as a personal matter. I think a person ought to be judged on how he or she lives his life, or lives her life. And that's how I've tried to live my life, through example. Faith-based is an important part of my life, individually, but I don't—*I don't ascribe a person's opposing my nominations to an issue of faith.*
Reporter:	Do you think that's an inappropriate statement? And what I asked is—
Bush:	No, I just don't agree with it.
Reporter:	You don't agree with it.
Bush:	No, *I think people oppose my nominees because—because of judicial philosophy.*
Reporter:	Sorry, I asked you what you think of the ways faith is being used *in our political debates*, not just *in society*—
Bush:	No, I know you asked me that. Well, I can only speak to myself [*sic*], and I am mindful that people in political office should not say to somebody, "You're not equally American if you don't happen to agree with my view of religion." As I said, I think faith is a personal issue, and I get great strength from my faith. But I don't condemn somebody in the political process because they may not agree with me on religion. The great thing about America, David, is that you should be allowed to worship any way you want, and if you choose not to worship, you're equally as patriotic as somebody who does worship. And if you choose to worship, you're equally American if you're a Christian, a Jew, a Muslim. That's the wonderful thing about our country, and that's the way it should be.

Apr. 28, 2005

The issue, of course, is that Bush is not nominating Jews or Muslims or atheists, but ultra-conservative Christians to judicial posts.

Finally, when asked by Diane Sawyer whether he believes God is behind him, Bush replied:

Sawyer:	One of the questions that I guess people have is, "Does your confidence come from feeling that—that God is behind you?"
Bush:	My confidence comes from a lot of sources. I do, I am sustained by the prayers of the people in this country. I guess an appropriate way to say this is—one of the beautiful things about America and Americans from all walks of life is that they're willing to pray for the President and his family. And that's powerful. It's hard for me to describe to you what that means. It's, let me just say this, it's a leap of faith to understand.

Dec. 16, 2003

Bush on Education

George W. Bush will be the first to tell you that he didn't get the most out of his college days at two top-rate institutions—Phillips Andover Academy and Yale. Unfortunately, little is known about his time at Andover. At Yale, however, he partied and socialized and blamed the snobbishness of the intellectual climate for his indifference to learning while there.

> I had fun at Yale. I got a lot of great friends out of Yale. And I didn't pay attention. I guess there were some people who paid attention, some of whom you've obviously been talking to. But I didn't want to be friends with these *people who felt superior.*

Bush has also been candid about his own distaste for reading. Consider an interview in the *New York Times* in 1988, which shows the pain with which Bush recalls being forced to read the classics.

> I had to read *War and Peace* when I was 16 or 17. Don't give me a quiz on the thousands of characters in it, but I guess it had an influence because it was a discipline. It was more that than remembering anything in it. And of course, we had to read Shakespere in school. It was required.

Oct. 27, 1988

In addition, as president, Bush has openly stated on more than one occasion that he gets his news not from reading papers, but from his advisory staff, who inform him of noteworthy events at the beginning of the day and throughout (see Bush's Dyslexia, chapter five).

Having squandered the opportunity for an exceptional college experience, Bush as president stands in sharp contrast to the many highly intellectual American presidents such as Thomas Jefferson, James Madison, Abraham Lincoln, Theodore Roosevelt, and even Bill Clinton, just prior to him. Mark Crisping Miller in *The Bush Dyslexicon* calls Bush "something of an anti-Lincoln", who, "instead of learning eagerly in humble circumstances, learned almost nothing at the finest institutions in the land".[3]

Overall, Bush's views on education mirror his indifference to learning as something potentially valuable in its own right. Thus, he also is something of an anti-Aristotelian. For Bush, learning is not valued in itself; it is worthwhile and only worthwhile insofar as it furthers one's business savvy and skills. Miller aptly adds:

> Bush's view of education is overfocused on "results"—a clear reflection of his fierce probusiness fundamentalism. Students must be educated for the workforce, and that's it. They must have the basic skills and solid "character" to be reliable employees and, therefore, energetic shoppers. Any higher instruction and they might turn "arrogant"—or "uppity," as some folks used to say.[4]

Given this, one is not surprised to find that Bush's No Child Left Behind Act focuses on "accountability for results", instead of learning as something valuable in itself. The NCLB law, signed in January of 2002, in effect pressures teachers not to teach, but to prepare students to be successful test-takers.

---

3 Mark Crispin Miller, *The Bush Dyslexicon: Observations on a National Disorder* (New York: W. W. Norton & Company, 2002), 14.

4 Mark Crispin Miller, *The Bush Dyslexicon,* 137

In the third debate with Kerry, Bush talked of the problem he had noticed that had served as a goad for his ideas of educational reform.

> And I saw a problem in the public education system in America. They were just shuffling too many kids through the system, year after year, grade after grade, without learning the basics. And so we said: Let's raise the standards. We're spending more money, but let's raise the standards and measure early and solve problems now, before it's too late. No, *education is how to help the person who's lost a job. Education is how to make sure we've got a workforce that's productive and competitive.* Got four more years, I've got more to do to continue to raise standards, to continue to reward teachers and school districts that are working, to emphasize math and science in the classrooms, to continue to expand Pell Grants to make sure that people have an opportunity to start their career with a college diploma.
>
> Oct. 13, 2004

What precisely is the No Child Left Behind Act? Bush had this to say at an address in Springfield, Ohio in 2004:

> So John [Boehner] and I and others drafted some legislation called the No Child Left Behind Act, the heart of which says the following things.
>
> One, we trust local people to make the right decisions for the schools. We're going to talk about some school decision-makers—with some school decision-makers here.
>
> Secondly, it says we need to measure, not the federal government doesn't need to measure, the people outside of Washington need to measure so we can determine whether or not we're meeting—meeting goals. And the first goal is every child reading by third grade—at grade-level by the third grade. It seems to make sense, doesn't it? That's a legitimate request to ask of the school systems, in return for 49 percent increase in K through 12 funding since I've been in Washington, D.C., that people learn how to read, write, add, and subtract.
>
> Thirdly, we're raising the standards. I went to Washington *to challenge the soft bigotry of low expectations.* What that means is, when you lower the standards, you get lousy results. We can't have a hopeful America unless every child has a chance to succeed because every child has been taught how to read and write and add and subtract. As a result of the legislation we passed, an achievement gap is beginning to close in this country.It's happening.

> I'll tell you what else we did, which is an important part of the accountability system. We—I'm going to use a fancy word— "disaggregated results" *[sic]*. That means we measured by race, for example. See, we want to know if every child is learning to read and write and add and subtract. We don't want any doubt in our mind that the system is making sure it's hopeful for everybody. You don't know whether every child is learning to read and write and add and subtract unless you measure, unless you show the results, unless you say to parents, "This school is great. This school needs help."
>
> Some people say, "You shouldn't test. You're just punishing the schools." I disagree. By not testing, you're punishing children. By testing, you can determine what needs to be—what needs to be cured. You can't solve a problem unless you diagnose the problem. And we're using the accountability system as a diagnostic tool to lift the sights and the spirits of every child in this country. So that's what we're here to talk about, the No Child Left Behind Act. It's a vital piece of legislation.
>
> Sept. 27, 2004

The rhetoric here strongly suggests that it takes a Texan to come to Washington to challenge the "soft bigotry of low expectations" and get something positive done.

When asked in Virginian a question about public and private education, Bush replied with some more soft-bigotry talk:

> Here's what we're going to do: We're going to continue to *challenge the soft bigotry of low expectations,* is what we're going to do. And by that, I mean—let me tell you what that means. That means, if you set the bar low, you're going to get lousy results. It starts with recognizing that every child can learn to read and write and add and subtract, and that we must not allow systems to develop that just shuffle kids through. That's what's happening, let's be frank about it. We had systems—school systems around this country that evidently didn't think certain kids could learn, so they just moved them on, you know? And guess what happened, when they came out at the end, they couldn't read. And everybody went, "Oops, what went wrong?"
>
> So we've changed that in Washington. We've increased federal funding. Title I money is up by 52 percent since I became the President. Elementary and—elementary and secondary school programs are up by 49 percent. Those are healthy increases in spending. But—well, there's more than just spending when it comes to schools. Now we're asking the question: Show us [*sic*]. See, for the first time the federal government is

> saying to school districts, "We expect to see results. We want our kids reading by—at grade level by the third grade". There's nothing wrong with asking [*sic*] that. It seems like a legitimate request.
>
> ...And so first thing we've done is we've changed the whole attitude toward public schools. It's an optimistic attitude. It says, "We know every child can read, and we expect every child to read, and, therefore, why don't you show us"? And if not, there will be extra help....
>
> Now, *we're making great progress on education.*
>
> North Virginia Community College, Aug. 9, 2004

Or consider these statements, which reveal his attitude toward learning with alarming bluntness:

> You teach a child to read, and *he or she will be able to pass a literacy test.*
>
> Townsend, TN, Feb. 21, 2001

> I want it to be said that *the Bush administration was a results-oriented administration*, because I believe the results of focusing our attention and energy on teaching children to read and having an education system that's responsive to the child and to the parents, as opposed to mired in a system that refuses to change, will make America what we want it to be—a literate country and a hopefuller [*sic*] country.
>
> Washington, D.C., Jan. 11, 2001

The following exchange between Bush and a reporter on Bush's No Child Left Behind at a press conference in April of 2005 is most revealing. The emphasis here, as it is always, is on *measurement.*

> Reporter: Mr. President, you've made No Child Left Behind a big part of your education agenda. The nation's largest teachers union has filed suit against it, saying it's woefully inadequately funded. What's your response to that? And do you think that No Child Left Behind is working?
>
> Bush: Yes, I think it's working. And the reason why I think it's working is because we're *measuring*, and the *measurement* is showing progress toward teaching people how to read and write and add and subtract. Listen, the whole theory behind No Child Left Behind is this: if we're going to spend federal money, we expect the states to show us

> whether or not we're achieving simple objectives—like literacy, literacy in math, the ability to read and write. And, yes, we're making progress. And I can say that with certainty because we're *measuring*, Richard.
>
> Look, I'm a former governor, I believe states ought to control their own destiny when it comes to schools. They are by far the biggest funder of education, and it should remain that way. But we spend a lot of money here at the federal level and have increased the money we spend here quite dramatically at the federal level. And we changed the policy: instead of just spending money and hope for the best, we're now spending money and saying, "*Measure*."
>
> And some people don't like to *measure*. But if you don't *measure*, how do you know whether or not you've got a problem in a classroom? I believe it's best to *measure* early and correct problems early, before it's too late. That's why as a part of the No Child Left Behind Act we had money available for remedial education. In other words, we said we're going to *measure*, and when we detect someone who needs extra help, that person will get extra help.
>
> But, absolutely, it's a good piece of legislation. I will do everything I can to prevent people from unwinding it, by the way.
>
> Apr. 28, 2005

Overall, Bush's unambiguous message is that learning is a matter of inputs and outputs, like some business transaction; it is not something that is inherently pleasurable. Consistent with Skinnerian functional analysis, education is a matter of conditioning organisms to behave in certain desirable ways and not others. Gone is the Aristotelian insistence that people have a natural curiosity and desire to learn. Gone is the wonder and beauty of learning for the sake of itself.

Section Two
Bush's Ethical Rhetoric

The Post:	Do you plan to expend any political capital to aggressively lobby senators for a gay marriage amendment?
Bush:	You know, I think that the situation in the last session—well, first of all, I do believe it's necessary; many in the Senate didn't, because they believe DOMA [the Defense of Marriage Act] will—is in place, but—they know DOMA is in place, and they're waiting to see whether or not DOMA will withstand a constitutional challenge.
The Post:	Do you plan on trying to—using the White House, using the bully pulpit, and trying to—
Bush:	The point is—is that senators have made it clear that so long as DOMA is deemed constitutional, nothing will happen. I'd take their admonition seriously.
The Post:	But until that changes, you want it?
Bush:	Well, until that changes, nothing will happen in the Senate. Do you see what I'm saying?
The Post:	Right.
Bush:	The logic?

Interview with *Washington Post*, Jan. 16, 2005

THIS SECTION TURNS TO ETHICAL ISSUES, which I break into two chapters: "Bush on Other-Concern" and "Know Thyself". The first chapter comprises issues such as moral absolutism, moral consequentialism, values, moral clarity, the “ethics” of war, and culpability. The second chapter comprises Bush’s own views on himself, leadership, manliness, “compassionate conservatism”, progress, and unity.

Chapter 4
Bush and Other-Concern

"'I like the Walrus best', said Alice: 'because you see he was a little *sorry for the poor oysters [he and the Carpenter ate]'.*

"'He ate more than the Carpenter, though', said Tweedledee. 'You see he held his handkerchief in front, so that the Carpenter couldn't count how many he took: contrariwise'.

"'That was mean!' Alice said indignantly. 'Then I like the Carpenter best—if he didn't eat so many as the Walrus'.

"'But he ate as many as he could get', said Tweedledum'.

"This was a puzzler. After a pause, Alice began, 'Well! They were both *very unpleasant characters—'"*

Moral Absolutism

For philosophers, *moral absolutism* is the view that there are universal moral truths, precepts, virtues, laws, or guidelines for human beings that are discoverable by rational reflection, moral intuition, or even intense empirical investigation.

As his frequent assertions make abundantly clear, Bush is himself an avowed absolutist. Values, he says with fundamentalist pride, are universal. A fine illustration of Bush's moral absolutism is his speech at West Point:

> Some worry that it is somehow undiplomatic or impolite to speak the language of right and wrong. I disagree. Different circumstances require different methods, but not different moralities. Moral truth is the same in every culture, in every time, and in every place. Targeting innocent civilians for murder is always and everywhere wrong. Brutality against women is always and everywhere wrong. There can be no neutrality between justice and cruelty, between the innocent and the guilty. We are in a conflict between good and evil, and America will call evil by its name. By confronting evil and lawless regimes, we do not create a problem, we reveal a problem. And we will lead the world in opposing it.

And again in the same address:

> The 20th century ended with a single surviving model of human progress, based on non-negotiable demands of human dignity, the rule of law, limits on the power of the state, respect for women and private property and free speech and equal justice and religious tolerance….
>
> When it comes to the common rights and needs of men and women, there is no clash of civilizations. The requirements of freedom apply fully to Africa and Latin America and the entire Islamic world. The peoples of the Islamic nations want and deserve the same freedoms and opportunities as people in every nation. And their governments should listen to their hopes. A truly strong nation will permit legal avenues of dissent for all groups that pursue their aspirations without violence. An advancing nation will pursue economic reform, to unleash the great entrepreneurial energy of its people. A thriving nation will respect the rights of women, because no society can prosper while denying opportunity to half its citizens. *Mothers and fathers and children across the Islamic world, and all the world* [sic], *share the same fears and aspirations.* In poverty, they struggle. In tyranny, they suffer. And as we saw in Afghanistan, in liberation they celebrate.
>
> June 1, 2002

Bush makes the same point in his second Inaugural Address in 2005.

> Across the generations we have proclaimed the imperative of self-government, because no one is fit to be a master and no one deserves to be a slave….
>
> Americans move forward in every generation by reaffirming *all that is good and true that came before—ideals of justice and conduct that are the same yesterday, today, and forever.*
>
> Inaugural Address, Jan. 20, 2005

At an early speech at Bob Jones University, an anti-Catholic evangelical school that has banned inter-racial dating—Bush tells his audience that values are universal in that they are given to men from God.

> Unique among the nations, America recognized *the source of our character as being godly and eternal,* not being civic and temporal. And because we have understood that our source is eternal, America has been different. We have no king by Jesus.... When you have no king but Jesus, you release the eternal, you release the highest and best, you release virtue, you release potential.
>
> May 8, 1999

Moreover, Americans, in full recognition that Jesus is the only king, are in fullest possession of eternality, goodness, virtue, and human potential.

Again in the address to the graduating West Point cadets, Bush explicitly claims, as he has done often before, that freedom is God's gift to all human beings.

> But we also understand that the way to defeat terror in the long run, the way to defeat hopelessness and despair, is to spread freedom and democracy. We understand that freedom is not America's gift to the world; *freedom is the Almighty God's gift to each man and woman in this world.*

It is, however, baffling that such a great gift has not been recognized by humans for centuries and is still not recognized by much of the globe today. In an interview with Tim Russert, Bush explains plainly that America and he have a calling to spread freedom.

> And, Tim, as you can tell, I've got a foreign policy that is one that believes *America has a responsibility in this world to lead*, a responsibility to lead in the war against terror, a responsibility to speak clearly about the threats that we all face, a responsibility to promote freedom, to free people from the clutches of barbaric people such as Saddam Hussein who tortured, mutilated—there were mass graves that we have found—a responsibility to fight AIDS, the pandemic of AIDS, and to

> feed the hungry. We have a responsibility. To me that is history's call to America. I accept the call and will continue to lead in that direction.
>
> *Meet the Press*, Feb. 7, 2004

And as the West Point speech shows, this calling is a *moral imperative* to act—again, the doctrine of *officium paci*.

> Building this just peace is America's opportunity, and *America's duty*.... America has no empire to extend or utopia to establish. We wish for others only what we wish for ourselves—safety from violence, the rewards of liberty, and the hope for a better life.

Moral Consequentialism

Moral consequentialism is the view that actions are judged moral or immoral insofar as they bring about favorable or unfavorable moral consequences and what is favorable is often cashed out in terms of pleasure, happiness, or goodness. Such a view is generally considered to be inconsistent with moral absolutism.[1]

Given the inconsistency between absolutism and consequentialism as they are generally construed today, there is a major difficulty with Bush's avowed absolutism. A careful look at Bush's addresses, interviews, and press conferences reveal a chameleon-like knack for jumping between absolutism and consequentialism to suit the moment. I begin with Bush's address to the United Nations in 2003.

> Helping Afghanistan and Iraq to succeed as free nations in a transformed region, cutting off the avenues of proliferation, abolishing modern forms of slavery—these are the kinds of great tasks for which the United Nations was founded. In each case, careful discussion is needed, and also decisive action. *Our good intentions will be credited only if we achieve good outcomes.*
>
> Sept. 23, 2003

---

1 One exception is Greek Stoicism, which argues what is absolutely good is also what is expedient and conversely what is expedient is what is good. See Cicero's *On Ends*.

Consider also this length reply to a question from moderator, Jim Lehrer, in first debate with John Kerry.

Lehrer: Has the war in Iraq been worth the cost of American lives, 1,052 as of today?

Bush: You know, *every life is precious. Every life matters.* You know, my hardest—the hardest part of the job is to know that I committed the troops in harm's way and then do the best I can to provide comfort for the loved ones who lost a son or a daughter or a husband or wife. You know, I think about Missy Johnson. She's a fantastic lady I met in Charlotte, North Carolina. She and her son Bryan, they came to see me. Her husband PJ got killed. He'd been in Afghanistan, went to Iraq. You know, it's hard work to try to love her as best as I can, knowing full well that the decision I made caused her loved one to be in harm's way. I told her after we prayed and teared up [*sic*] and laughed some that I thought her husband's sacrifice was noble and worthy. Because I understand the stakes of this war on terror. I understand that we must find Al Qaida wherever they hide. We must deal with threats before they fully materialize. And Saddam Hussein was a threat, and that we must spread liberty because in the long run, *the way to defeat hatred and tyranny and oppression is to spread freedom.* Missy understood that. That's what she told me her husband understood. So you say, "Was it worth it?" *Every life is precious.* That's what distinguishes us from the enemy. *Everybody matters. But I think it's worth it, Jim. I think it's worth it, because I think—I know in the long term a free Iraq, a free Afghanistan, will set such a powerful in a part of the world that's desperate for freedom. It will help change the world; that we can look back and say we did our duty.*

Every life is precious, Bush acknowledges, consistent with moral absolutism, but then he trumps this consequentially by appealing *vaguely* to the long-term benefits of a free Afghanistan and a free Iraq. Just what are these benefits that can so readily justify the loss of thousands of lives? He never clearly spells these out. Moreover, absolutism is not something to be trumped by an appeal to consequences. Thus, the confusion in his thinking is manifest.

In a press conference in 2005, Bush sweeps away issues about the gross numbers of troops put in harm's way by appealing, as is his wont, to perceived long-term consequences of the occupation of Iraq. In doing so, he repeats what have become two irritating mantras: *The world is better off without Saddam Hussein* and *We're making progress.*

> Reporter: The army says that we'll probably have 100,000 or more troops in Iraq for at least another year. What would you say to the American people, including a significant number who supported you at the beginning of the war, who now say this is not what we were led to believe would happen?
>
> Bush: A couple of things, John. I'd say the world is better off without Saddam Hussein in power. A world with Saddam Hussein in power would have been a—would have been a more dangerous world today. Secondly, that we're making progress in helping Iraq develop a democracy. And in the long-term, our children and grandchildren will benefit from a free Iraq.
>
> Jan. 26, 2005

Of course, the main problem with these tiresome consequentialist claims is, as used, they appeal to the indefinitely vague future. As such, if Iraq at any time in the indefinite future—say even 100 years from now—becomes a prosperous and stable nation, one could claim both that this turn of events was ultimately brought about by the American invasion in 2003 and that Bush, God's own ambassador for peace, was the catalyst for stability.

Finally, I give a line on the death penalty, which Bush justifies consequentially.

> I still support the death penalty, and I think it's a deterrent to crime.
>
> Mar. 16, 2005

Such an argument seems especially astonishing, when we consider that George W. Bush is a president who maintains flatly "every life matters".

Bush on Values

Bush's notion of "values" has a Texas flavor—specifically a Crawford, Texas, flavor—as if Crawford's values are those of America.

> I do want to remind you all that one of the things that makes this country so unique [*sic*] is our value system: the values of hard work, family, faith—values that sound pretty much like the heartland of America to me.... But it's important for all of us in Washington to stay in touch with the values of the heartland because they're values that really are unique. It basically says that values—a value system of basic inherent values that override politics and different demographies and different religions. It's what makes America so unique and great.
>
> July 27, 2001

Precisely what this means, of course, is anyone's guess. Bush seems to be saying that the universally recognizable values that are given to men by God are most easily discovered in "the heartland". Again, in this reference to Scouting:

> And whenever I go home to the heartland, I am reminded of the values that build strong families, strong communities and strong character—the values that make our people unique. Every society depends on trust and loyalty, on courtesy and kindness, on bravery and reverence. These are the values of Scouting and these are the values of America.
>
> July 30, 2001

In West Virginia, Bush said that America's actions abroad are value-based.

> And there's no doubt in my mind, when the United States acts abroad and home, *we do so based upon values—particularly the value that we hold dear to our hearts, and that is, everybody ought to be free.* I want to repeat what I said during my State of the Union to you. Liberty is not America's gift to the world. What we believe strongly, and what we hold dear, is liberty is God's gift to mankind. And we hold that value precious. And we believe it is true.
>
> White Sulphur Springs, Feb. 9, 2003

The implication is that the U.S. is incapable of or unlikely to err when it acts abroad. America is, after all, only spreading liberty.

And let us not forget America's high regard for rights and human dignity.

> My trip today [to Germany] should say to the people of this good country and my country that past disagreements are behind us, and we're moving forward for the good of mankind. And that shouldn't be a surprise to people, because we believe in human rights and human dignity and the worth of every individual.
>
> Mainz, Germany, Feb. 23, 2005

Following the consequentialist strain in his ethical thinking, Bush explains in an address to black leaders at the Indiana Black Exposition that ownership is one of the keys to securing American values.

> To ensure that the promise of America reaches all our citizens, we're working to build an ownership society in which more of our citizens have a personal stake in the future of our country. *When you own something*, your life is more secure. *When you own something*, you have more dignity. *When you own something*, you have greater independence. *The more people who own something in America* means this country is better off. So we've been working to promote an ownership society.
>
> July 14, 2005

Bush on Moral Clarity

The challenges that confront America with its *officium paci* doctrine are numerous. So too are the responsibilities. They require sufficient moral purpose, vision, and character. In short, they require moral clarity. In his West Point address, Bush talks of the moral clarity of presidents Kennedy and Reagan, who paved the route for the Cold-War victory against Soviet Russia.

> America confronted imperial communism in many different ways—diplomatic, economic, and military. Yet moral clarity was essential to our victory in the Cold War. When leaders like John F. Kennedy and Ronald Reagan

> refused to gloss over the brutality of tyrants, they gave hope to prisoners and dissidents and exiles, and rallied free nations to a great cause.
>
> June 1, 2002

In an address to the United Nations, Bush appeals to the moral clarity of member nations in helping to free Afghanistan and Iraq.

> All the challenges I have spoken of this morning require urgent attention and moral clarity. Helping Afghanistan and Iraq to succeed as free nations in a transformed region, cutting off the avenues of proliferation, abolishing modern forms of slavery—these are the kinds of great tasks for which the United Nations was founded. In each case, careful discussion is needed, and also decisive action.
>
> Address to United Nations, Sept. 23, 2003

Here, at the end of the day, one cannot help but wonder whether "moral clarity" just means being in complete agreement with the United States on how to handle the situation in the Middle East.

Bush on Culpability

Before becoming president, Bush campaigned aggressively on the issue of accountability. He even had a campaign plane, used in the 2000 election, dubbed "Responsibility One"—though as we shall see he has been anything but accountable the whole of his political career.

First, in an interview with National Public Radio about the 152 persons that he'd sent to their death while governor of Texas, Bush replied with alarming confidence:

> The only thing that I can tell you is that every case I have reviewed, I have been comfortable with the innocence or guilt of the person that I've looked at. I do not believe we've put a guilty [oops!]—I mean, innocent person to death in the state of Texas.
>
> *All Things Considered*, NPR, June 16, 2000

During the chaos of the Florida vote recount, Bush was asked at a press briefing why he went forth and sought an injunction in Florida. He replied, as would any fully accountable candidate:

> I think *you ought to call Jim Baker and let him—he made the explanation today,* and I thought it was very sound and reasoned explanation. And if you've got any further comment—questions about that—just call him—call his office. He'll be the person in charge of explaining our position as to why we don't think there needs to be three elections.
>
> Nov. 11, 2000

In October of 2003, Bush fielded a question from a reporter about what his administration knew about 9/11, prior to it.

> Reporter: Mr. President, thank you. As you know, the Chairman of the commission investigating the September 11th attacks wants documents from the White House, and said this week that he might have to use subpoena power. You have said there's some national security concerns about turning over some of those documents to people outside of the Executive Branch. Will you turn them over, or can you at least outline for the American people what you think is a reasonable compromise so that the commission learns what it needs to know, and you protect national security, if you think it's that important?
>
> Bush: Yes. It is important for me to protect national security. You're talking about the presidential daily brief. It's important for the writers of the presidential daily brief to feel comfortable that the documents will never be politicized and/or unnecessarily exposed for public purview. *I—and so, therefore, the kind of—the first statements out of this administration were very protective of the presidential prerogatives of the past and to protect the right for other presidents, future presidents, to have a good presidential daily brief.*
>
> Oct. 28, 2003

In the same press conference, when Bush was asked whether his war-is-over comments aboard the USS Abraham Lincoln were "premature", he responded aggressively, as he typically does when caught in a lie:

Reporter: Mr. President, if I may take you back to May 1st when you stood on the USS Lincoln under a huge banner that said, "Mission Accomplished". At that time you declared major combat operations were over, but since that time there have been over 1,000 wounded, many of them amputees who are recovering at Walter Reed, 217 killed in action since that date. Will you acknowledge now that you were premature in making those remarks?

Bush: Nora, *I think you ought to look at my speech. I said, Iraq is a dangerous place and we've still got hard work to do, there's still more to be done.* And we had just come off a very successful military operation. I was there to thank the troops. The "Mission Accomplished" sign, of course, was put up by the members of the USS Abraham Lincoln, saying that their mission was accomplished. I know it was attributed some how to some ingenious advance man from my staff—they weren't that ingenious, by the way. But *my statement was a clear statement, basically recognizing that this phase of the war for Iraq was over and there was a lot of dangerous work.* And *it's proved to be right*, it is dangerous in Iraq. It's dangerous in Iraq because there are people who can't stand the thought of a free and peaceful Iraq. It is dangerous in Iraq because there are some who believe that we're soft, that the will of the United States can be shaken by suiciders—and suiciders who are willing to drive up to a Red Cross center, a center of international help and aid and comfort, and just kill.

Oct. 28, 2003

An examination of his speech (see chapter one, pp. 15-6) reveals clearly that his comments were indeed premature, if not misleading or false.

In this exchange at a press conference in 2004, Bush seems to grow irate with a reporter, who presses him on the issue of responsibility for the events of 9/11.

Reporter: Thank you, Mr. President. Two weeks ago, a former counterterrorism official at the NSC, Richard Clarke, offered an unequivocal apology to the American people for failing them prior to 9-11. Do you believe the American people deserve a similar apology from you, and would you prepared to give them one?

Bush: Look, I can understand why people in my administration are anguished over the fact that people lost their life. I feel the same way. I mean, I'm sick when I think about the death that took place on that day. And as I mentioned, I've met with a lot of family members, and I do the best to console them about the loss of their loved one.

As I mentioned, I oftentimes think about what I could have done differently. I can assure the American people that had we had any inkling that this was going to happen, we would have done everything in our power to stop the attack. Here's what I feel about that: *The person responsible for the attacks was Osama bin Laden. That's who's responsible for killing Americans. And that's why we will stay on the offense until we bring people to justice.*

April 13, 2004

At the same press conference, Bush again is pressed on any post-9/11 mistakes that he might have made as president by another reporter. After initial confusion, he responds with many of the same old platitudes, and then ends as confused as he began.

Reporter: Thank you, Mr. President. In the last campaign, you were asked a question about the biggest mistake you'd made in your life, and you used to like to joke that it was trading Sammy Sosa. You've looked back before 9/11 for what mistakes might have been made. After 9/11, what would your biggest mistake be, would you say, and what lessons have learned from it?

Bush: I wish you'd have given me this written question ahead of time so I could plan for it. John, I'm sure historians will look back and say, "Gosh, he could've done it better this way or that way". You know, I just—I'm sure something will pop into my head here in the midst of this press conference, with all the pressure of trying to come up with answer, but it hadn't yet.

I would've gone into Afghanistan the way we went into Afghanistan. Even knowing what I know today about the stockpiles of weapons, I still would've called upon the world to deal with Saddam Hussein. See, I'm of the belief that *we'll find out the truth on the weapons.* That's why we sent up the independent commission. I look forward to

> hearing the truth as to exactly where they are. *They could still be there.* They could be hidden, like the 50 tons of mustard gas in a turkey farm....
>
> But it'll all settle out, John. We'll find out the truth about the weapons at some point in time. However, the fact that *he had the capacity to make* them bothers me today just like it would have bothered me then. *He's a dangerous man. He's a man who actually not only had weapons of mass destruction—the reason I can say that with certainty is because he used them. And I have no doubt in my mind that he would like to have inflicted harm, or paid people to inflict harm, or trained people to inflict harm, on America, because he hated us.*
>
> I hope—I don't want to sound like I have made no mistakes. I'm confident I have. I just haven't—you just put me under the spot here, and maybe I'm not as quick on my feet as I should be in coming up with one.
>
> Apr. 13, 2004

Through it all, the painful mental exercise of trying to think up one post-9/11 mistake in his presidency proves a task too difficult.

Next consider what Bush said about sharing his administration's policies with Congress and the public in general.

> Reporter: Given that you've not convinced everyone in your own party of that [that Bush's administration freely shares information on its energy policy with Congress], to what degree are you trying to recalibrate the power between Congress and the presidency?
>
> Bush: First of all, I'm not going to let Congress erode the power of the executive branch. I have a duty to protect the executive branch from legislative encroachment. I mean, for example, when the GAO demands documents from us, we're not going to give them to them. I mean, it's just, you know—these were privileged conversations. These were conversations when people come into our offices and brief us. And can you imagine having to give up every single transcript of what [*sic*] has advised me or the vice president? Our advice wouldn't be good and honest and open. And so I viewed that as an encroachment on the power of

> the executive branch. I have an obligation to make sure that the presidency remains robust and that the legislative branch doesn't end up running the executive branch.
>
> Mar. 13, 2002

In the second debate with John Kerry, Bush was asked to list three mistakes he had made in his political career. Similar to the press conference of April 13 of 2004, the task proved too formidable.

> I have made a lot of decisions, and some of them little, like appointments to boards you never heard of, and some of them big. And in a war, there's a lot of—there's a lot of tactical decisions that historians will look back and say: He shouldn't have done that. He shouldn't have made that decision. And I'll take responsibility for them. I'm human. But *on the big questions, about whether or not we should have gone into Afghanistan, the big question about whether we should have removed somebody in Iraq, I'll stand by those decisions, because I think they're right. That's really what you're—when they ask about the mistakes, that's [*sic*] what they're talking about. They're trying to say, "Did you make a mistake going into Iraq?" And the answer is, "Absolutely not". It was the right decision.* The Duelfer report confirmed that decision today, because what Saddam Hussein was doing was trying to get rid of sanctions so he could reconstitute a weapons program. And the biggest threat facing America is terrorists with weapons of mass destruction. We knew he hated us. We knew he'd been—invaded other countries. We knew he tortured his own people. On the tax cut, it's a big decision. *I did [*sic*] the right decision.* Our recession was one of the shallowest in modern history. Now, you asked, "What mistakes?" I made some mistakes in appointing people, but I'm not going to name them. I don't want to hurt their feelings on national TV. But history will look back, and I'm fully prepared to accept any mistakes that history judges to my administration, because the president makes the decisions, the president has to take the responsibility.
>
> Oct. 8, 2004

In short, Bush is fully prepared to accept the verdict of history on the big questions, like the war with Iraq, because, as only he can put it, "I did the right decision".

Of course, the administration eventually did grudgingly concede that there were major intelligence errors prior to going into Iraq. When asked by members of *The Washington Post* why no one in the administration was held accountable for the faulty intelligence on weapons of mass destruction in Iraq, Bush answered evasively, but decisively.

> Well, we had an accountability moment, and that's called the 2004 election. And the American people listened to different assessments made about what was taking place in Iraq, and they looked at the two candidates, and chose me, for which I'm grateful.
>
> Jan. 16, 2005

Two months later, a reporter asked whether Bush felt vindicated with certain emerging signs of democratization of Iraq.

> Reporter: Mr. President, you faced a lot of skepticism in the run-up to the Iraq war, and a lot of criticism for miscalculating some of the challenges of postwar Iraq. Now that the Iraq elections seem to be triggering signs of democratization throughout the broader Middle East, do you feel any sense of vindication?
>
> Bush: First of all, I fully understand that as long as I'm the President I will face criticism. It's like part of the job. Frankly, you wouldn't be doing your job if you didn't occasionally lay out the gentle criticism. I welcome constructive ideas as to how we might do our job better. So that doesn't bother me. *And, therefore, since it doesn't bother me and I expect it, I don't then seek vindication.*
>
> Mar. 16, 2005

In response to the suggestion that he was violating international law in not letting Germany and France invest in post-war Iraq, Bush quipped sarcastically:

> International law? I better call my lawyer!
>
> *Washington Post*, Dec. 12, 2003

Finally, there's the Karl Rove/Valerie Plame scandal. Plame's husband, Joe Wilson, was sent on a mission to Niger in February of 2002 to investigate the legitimacy of a rumor that Hussein had tried to buy uranium for nuclear weapons. Wilson reported back that the rumor was likely false. Still, the "rumor" eventually found its way into Bush's State of the Union speech of January 28 of 2003 ("The British government has learned that Saddam Hussein recently sought significant quantities of uranium from Africa. Our intelligence sources tell us that he has attempted to purchase high-strength aluminum tubes suitable for nuclear weapons production"). On June 12 of 2003, *The Washington Post* reported that an unnamed ambassador to Africa [i.e., Wilson] said that the Niger episode was likely a fabrication. The administration was furious.

On July 14 of 2003 came payback. Conservative columnist Bob Novak wrote, "Wilson never worked for the CIA, but his wife, Valerie Plame, is an Agency operative on weapons of mass destruction. Two senior administration officials told me Wilson's wife suggested sending him to Niger…". This, in effect, blew Plame's cover, cost Plame her job, and endangered her life, but it sent a clear signal that the Bush administration would not be second-guessed. Rove, it seems, was one of the "leakers".

On June 10 of 2004, Bush was asked in a press conference about this leak. The exchange went as follows:

Reporter:	Given—given recent developments in the CIA leak case, particularly Vice President Cheney's discussions with the investigators, do you still stand by what you said several months ago, a suggestion that it might be difficult to identify anybody who leaked the agent's name?
Bush:	That's up to—
Reporter:	And, and, do you stand by your pledge to fire anyone found to have done so?
Bush:	*Yes*. And that's up to the U.S. Attorney to find the facts.
Reporter:	My final point would be—or question would be, has Vice President Cheney assured you—
Bush:	It's up to the—
Reporter:	—subsequent to his conversations with them, that nobody—
Bush:	I haven't talked to the Vice President about this matter, and I suggest—recently—and I suggest you talk to the U.S. Attorney about that. Hold on for a minute. I'm kind of

> observing for a second. I've got to call on the Texas newspaper. Hillman.

Here Bush unequivocally pledges to fire anyone who leaked Plame's name to the press. However, as it came out later that Rove did leak Plame's name to the press, the debate now centered on whether doing so was itself a crime. On July 18 of 2005, Bush characteristically changed his tune. No longer was leaking sufficient cause for firing, the "leaker" must be shown to have committed some crime. Going back on his word, Bush said, "[I]f someone *committed a crime*, they will no longer work in my administration".

What I take this section to have shown is that Bush perceives himself to be a take-charge president who can assume responsibility for all of his actions because he perceives that his intuitions on what's right for America and what's right for the world are unmistakable. Even if they are not, well, you see, he's still the president. As he said in an interview with Bob Woodward in 2002:

> I'm the commander, see. I don't need to explain—I do not need to explain why I say things. That's the interesting thing about being the President—maybe somebody needs to explain to me why they say something, but I don't feel like I owe anybody an explanation.

This says it all!

The "Ethics" of War

Moral absolutists in the mold of Mohandas Ghandi maintain that the notion of a right or just war is oxymoronic. Moral consequentialists argue for criteria *jus ad bellum* (criteria for the justice of going to war) and *jus in bello* (the criteria of justice while engaged in war). Is there an ethics of war?

My own thoughts are that war is always and everywhere morally inexcusable. Nonetheless, at least for the foreseeable future, war seems inevitable. And so, in this section, let us concern ourselves here only with *jus ad bellum*. Writes Andrew Valls:

> A just cause for a war is usually a defensive one. That is, a state is taken to have a just cause when it defends itself against aggression, where *aggression* means the violation or the imminent threat of the violation of its territorial integrity or political independence. So the just cause provision of just war theory holds, roughly, that the state has a right to defend itself against the aggression of other states.[2]

As we note above, though Bush is a moral absolutist at bottom, he seems to be consequentialist about war—especially since the events of 9/11 have given him moral clarity on ethical issues that too few are privileged to possess. Is there a way to square the tension?

Sadly, I think not. Certain quotes on war, prior to 9/11, set the stage for Bush's *officium paci* policy and betray colossal confusion in his mind on the rationale for war—*jus ad bellum*. Consider these harebrained quotes, prior to 9/11, on the proper reason for going to war.

> We ought to have a commander in chief who understands how to earn the respect of the military, by setting a clear mission, which is to win and fight war, *and therefore deter war.*
>
> *This Week*, ABC, Jan. 23, 2000

> The mission of the military is to fight and be able to win war, and *therefore prevent war from happening in the first place.*
>
> GOP Debate, Feb. 15, 2000

> I'm worried about the fact that our mission is not clear. It ought to be to have a military that's properly trained and equipped to be able to fight and win war, *and, therefore, prevent war from happening in the first place.*
>
> Nov. 3, 2000

---

2 Andrew Valls, "Can Terrorism Be Justified?", *Ethics in International Affairs: Theories and Cases* (New York: Rowman & Littlefield Publishers, Inc., 2000), 68.

Consider also these two nonsensical gems.

> Russia is no longer our enemy and therefore we shouldn't be locked into a Cold War mentality that says, "We keep the peace by blowing each other up".
>
> June 8, 2001

> I just want you to know that, when we talk about war, we're really talking about peace.
>
> June 18, 2002

Nonetheless, prior to 9/11, Bush's foreign policy, perhaps due to his inexperience with global politics, was fairly isolationist. He was also relatively shy about America's use of its military in global affairs. Consider these quotes from the second Bush/Gore debate.

> I'm worried about over-committing our military around the world. I want to be judicious in its use.

> I think what we need to do is convince people who live in the lands they live in to build the nations. Maybe I'm missing something here. I mean, we're going to have kind of a nation building core from America? Absolutely not! Our military is meant to fight and win war. That's what it's meant to do. And when it gets overextended, morale drops. I strongly believe we need to have a military presence in the peninsula, not only to keep the peace in the peninsula, but to keep regional stability. And I strongly believe we need to keep a presence in NATO, but I'm going to be judicious as to how to use the military. It needs to be in our vital interest, the mission needs to be clear, and the extra [exit] strategy obvious.
>
> Oct. 11, 2000

Yet the terrorists' activities of 9/11 changed everything. They offered him a sufficient justification for his invasion of Iraq. I begin with a press conference in March of 2002, where the reply Bush gives to a question about 9/11 is comical in its ignorance of events leading up to it.

> *We're a peaceful nation, and you know we're moving along just right and kind of having a—you know—time, and all of a sudden we get*

> *attacked.* And now we're at war, but we're at war to keep the peace. And it's very important for people in America to understand my attitude on this—that we're not out to seek revenge. Sure we're after justice. But I also view this as a really good opportunity to create a lasting peace.
>
> Mar. 13, 2002

Prior to this and not long after 9/11 itself, he says:

> We're also a nation that is adjusting to a new type of war. This isn't a conventional war that we're waging. Ours is a campaign that will have to reflect the new enemy. There's no longer islands [*sic*] to conquer or beachheads to storm. We face a brand of evil, the likes of which we haven't seen in a long time in the world. These are people who strike and hide, people who know no borders, people who are—people who depend upon others. And make no mistake about it, the new war is not only against the evildoers, themselves; the new war is against those who harbor them and finance them and feed them.
>
> Sept. 27, 2001

An exchange with Diane Sawyer shows that war for Bush goes beyond American security.

> Sawyer: Is there ever a point at which you would say, "this is too many, this is too high a price to be paying" [for war with Iraq]?
>
> Bush: My job is to do everything I can to protect America and Americans. We are at war. And the war on terror is—is the challenge of the 21st century. And we must win the war. And there are different fronts on the war on terror. And I will continue to do what I think is necessary to win that war. I—and the key for me is to remind the loved ones that *their troops are getting what is necessary to achieve the objective*, that this government's supporting them. And that we honor their memories, and *we will not stop short of the objective until we have achieved the objective.* The way to dishonor a memory of a fallen soldier is to quit too early, is to not to see that America is a more secure country and the world is a more peaceful place.
>
> Dec. 16, 2003

There is pronounced ethical tension here. Security means keeping citizens safe from harm, but war itself exposes some substantial subset of the citizens to harm. Clearly, for Bush, the number of casualties is irrelevant; it takes a back seat to war's objective—winning. This reveals a Lombardian approach to war that elevates attaining the objective above the means to attaining it. In a sense, what one is fighting for gets lost in the fight itself. Winning takes the place of the principle behind it.

Sawyer continues to press.

Sawyer: I guess for the family, how, maybe the question they would ask is, "How much do you suffer with each death?"

Bush: I—I—I'm—I can't imagine what it would be like to lose a son or a daughter or a husband, and—or a wife, for that matter. And I—it pains me.

Sawyer: Will we have fewer troops in Iraq this time next year?

Bush: That depends on the commanders on the ground. And it's very important for you to understand how I think the Commander in Chief ought to run a war and a reconstruction effort. *My job is to set the goal and to make sure our troops and planners have got the resources necessary to achieve the goal.*

Bush slips away from what many other writers acknowledge to be a most uncomfortable subject for him—empathy—to that which he's most comfortable talking about—achieving victory in war. He stammers uncomfortably with the first question, but his reply to the latter is stammer-free and confident.

Bush was pushed in a June 10 press conference of 2004 on the U.S.'s use of torture on Iraqi prisoners. At one point in the conference, a reporter asked him a moral question on torture in war. Bush snapped back tersely, rudely, and angrily in a manner that shows no sensitivity to the subtleties of moral discourse.

Reporter: Mr. President, I wanted to return to the question of torture. What we've learned from these memos this week is that the Department of Justice lawyers and the Pentagon lawyers have essentially worked out a way that U.S. officials can torture detainees without running afoul of the law. So when you say that you want the U.S. to adhere to international and U.S. laws, that's not very comforting. This is a moral question: Is torture ever justified?

Bush: Look, I'm going to say it one more time. If I—maybe—maybe I can be more clear. The instructions went out to our people to adhere to law. That ought to comfort you. We're a nation of law. We adhere to laws. We have laws on the books. You might look at those laws, and that might provide comfort for you. And those were the instructions out of—from me to the government.

Overall, there seems to be only one way to justify Bush's moral absolutism with his consequentialist attitude toward war. The motivation behind *officium paci* is god-sent. God has given Bush a clear moral message through the events of 9/11 that it is his and America's role to spread Texas-styled values across the globe. If so, this proves Osama bin Ladin correct: The war he has waged is truly a *jihad*. Religiosity is not at war with secularism; Islam is at war with Christianity.

Bush on the Environment

The environment has always been an issue largely ignored by Bush, as his initiatives have been prioritized toward economic stability and growth. In a press conference in Madrid, Spain, he argues that his refusal to endorse the Kyoto treaty is based in part on scientifically based suspicions that global warming is not caused by depleted ozone.

> I also said [in a statement yesterday] our nation is willing to continue to spend money on science, to make sure that any collective approach is one based upon sound science. I did speak out against the Kyoto Treaty itself, because I felt that the Kyoto Treaty was unrealistic, *it was not based upon science. The stated mandates in the Kyoto Treaty would affect our economy in a negative way.*

Later he would add:

> I come to the conference believing that every leader is sincere about their desire to clean the world—and so are we. *We have a different approach*, but we have the same goals. As I said earlier, I believe the Kyoto Treaty is a flawed treaty. I think that *it set unscientific goals*; it didn't include developing countries. On the other hand, I want to reiterate today, and I will do so throughout the week, that *we're committed to reducing greenhouse gases in the United States.*
>
> June 12, 2001

At a press conference with Vladamir Putin one month later in Genoa, Italy, Bush emphasizes that whatever plan he intends to put forth, it will not be such as to slow the economic growth of the United States.

> [M]y administration has had a full-scale review of the climate issue; that we're in the process of developing a strategy as quickly as we possibly can and one that we look forward to sharing with our friends and allies. A strategy that begins with the notion that we want to reduce greenhouse gasses in America. A strategy, also, that takes a realistic look at how best to do so, *a look based upon science* and a look with a notion that *we can have economic growth and sound environmental policy.* I made it clear to our friends and allies that the methodology of the current protocol is one that, if implemented, would severely affect economic growth in America, and that I believe that it makes sense for those who trade with us *to make sure that our environmental policy is one that continues to stimulate economic activity so that trade means something between nations.* The spirit of our dialogue was very positive. I guess you could say that I broke the ice during my last trip to Europe, so people understood exactly where I was coming from. There should be no doubt in their mind about our position—that we share the goal, but we believe that, strongly believe that *we need to find a methodology of achieving the goal that won't wreck the U.S. economy.*
>
> July 22, 2001

The Bush plan, of course, asked for voluntary restrictions on pollutants—that is, no plan at all.

More recently, when asked how the need for independence from the Gulf region is impacting the U.S.'s relationship with Russia, Bush replied:

> The best way to diversify, at least for my country—and I don't want to raise a sore subject here—but diversify away from dependence on foreign sources of energy, is for us to take advantage of new technologies and expand safe nuclear power in the United States of America. To me, that would achieve several objectives. One, it's a renewable source of energy; two, it's a domestic source of energy; and three, it would help us meet our obligations to clean air requirements. Unfortunately, it's an issue that's hard to get through our Congress. I mean, there's a lot [*sic*] of people still fearful of nuclear power, and it's a debate I've engaged in. It's a subject I brought up in my State of the Union address, and it's a subject I'll continue to talk about, because I think it is a way for the United States to be less dependent on foreign sources of energy, which is good for our economy, and, frankly, helps us with foreign policy.
>
> Mainz, Germany, Feb. 23, 2005

The third advantage is clearly absurd. Cleaner air would come about through dumping dangerous nuclear waste into the ground that cannot be secured in the long term.

Chapter 5
"Know Thyself"

"'"Who in the world am I?" Ah, that's the great puzzle!'"

Bush on Bush

The oracle at Delphi, the most famous oracle in antiquity, had inscribed on a wall the now-famous phrase *gnothi seauton*—that is, "know thyself".

> [This] inscription, early in Greek culture, was likely an injunction that meant each person should know his limitations as a human being—that is, no mortal should strive for godhood.... With the influence of philosophical investigation somewhat later, it came to enjoin self-reflection and self-understanding.[1]

Conquest of oneself through self-knowledge was a staple of much of Greek philosophy and a not-so-unreasonable one.

---

[1] M. Andrew Holowchak, *Happiness and Greek Ethics* (London: Continuum, 2002), xxi.

On superficial analysis, George W. Bush gives the impression that he is a man that knows who he and what it is he wants. Yet impressions are often very misleading.

I begin this section below with a quote from Bush, who's responding to a comment he made years ago that said in effect only Christians go to heaven. In typical fashion, Bush blames his critics for not taking what he said in its full context and then offers "the full story". The explanation does nothing to bail him out. He ends with a revealing slip: "I'm focused on me."

> I think that we're all God's children, and far be it from me, as a lowly sinner, trying to decide who gets to go to heaven and who doesn't, for example. I mean at one time, in 1994, I said, "My faith says you must accept Christ to go to heaven". And there was a significant backlash because, as typical in politics, *the full story wasn't told.* And there was a typical backlash amongst, you know, some Jewish people in Texas that basically felt I had said that they can't go to heaven. I worked hard to make it clear to people, far be it from me to tell you I get to decide who goes. I'm working on myself. *I'm focused on me.*
>
> Beliefnet.com, 2000

Before becoming president, Bush campaigned heavily on not being one of those "of-Washington" guys.

> Look, I fully recognize I'm not of Washington [*sic*]. I'm from Texas. And he's [Gore] got a lot of experience, but so do I. And I've been the chief executive officer of the second biggest state in the union. I have a proud record of working with both Republicans and Democrats, which is what our nation needs.
>
> Bush/Gore I, Oct. 3, 2000

> Lehrer: EITC?
> Bush: The Earned Income Tax Credit, sorry.
> Lehrer: That's all right.
> Bush: A lot of initials from a guy who's not from Washington, isn't it?
>
> Bush/Gore II, Oct. 11, 2000

> I trust people. I don't trust the federal government. It's going to be one of the themes you hear tonight. I don't want the federal government

> making decisions on behalf of everybody. There is an issue with the uninsured, there sure is. And we have uninsured people in my state. Ours is a big state, a fast-growing state. We share a common border with another nation. But we're providing health care for our people. One thing about "insurance", that's a Washington term.
>
> Bush/Gore III, Oct. 17, 2000

> And so, yeah, sometimes I agree with some of these groups in Washington and sometimes I don't. I'm a pretty independent thinker.
>
> Bush/Gore III, Oct. 17, 2000

As an "independent thinker", Bush vaunts that he is not swayed by polls or focus groups, when it comes to making decisions on behalf of the American people. In an address to Pittsburgh steelworkers at a picnic, he said:

> We don't stick our finger in the air to figure out which way the wind is blowing. I don't need a poll or focus group to tell me what to think. I do what I think is right for the American people. And we'll just let the political chips fall where they may.
>
> Aug. 26, 2001

Three days earlier, children and members of the press at Crawford Elementary School got the same message.

> If you're one of these types of people that are always trying to figure out which way the wind is blowing, decision-making can be difficult. But I find that—*I know who I am. I know what I believe in, and I know where I want to lead the country. And most of the decisions come pretty easily for me, to be frank with you.*
>
> Aug. 23, 2001

In a disingenuous attempt to show that he is indeed capable of feeling the pain of the relatives, loved ones, and friends of those who have died in the atrocities of 9/11, Bush says:

> There's only one person who hugs the mothers and the widows, the wives and the kids upon the death of their loved one. Others hug, but having committed the troops, I've got an additional responsibility to hug and that's me and I know what it's like.
>
> Dec. 11, 2002

More recently, Bush tries to explain to a reporter why Washington's atmosphere is so poisonously "partisan", when Bush is self-reputed to be the person who can bring "Democrats and Republicans together" (see "The Uniter", below).

Reporter: Sir, you've talked all around the country about the poisonous partisan atmosphere here in Washington. I wonder why do you think that is? And do you personally bear any responsibility in having contributed to this atmosphere?

Bush: I'm sure there are some people that don't like me. You know, Ed, I don't know. I've thought long and hard about it. I was—I've been disappointed. I felt that people could work—work together in good faith. It's just a lot of politics in the town. It's kind of a zero-sum attitude. We can't—we can't cooperate with so-and-so because it may make their party look good, and vice-versa.

Although having said that, we did have some success in the education bill. We certainly came together as a country after September the 11th. I appreciate the strong bipartisan support for supporting our troops in harm's way. There's been [*sic*] a lot of instances of bipartisanship, but when you bring a tough issue up like Social Security, it—sometimes people divide into camps.

I'm proud of my party. *Our party has been the party of ideas. We said, "Here's a problem, and here's some ideas [*sic*] as to how to fix it"*. And as I've explained to some people, I don't want to politicize this issue—people say, "You didn't need to bring this up, Mr. President, it may cost you politically". I don't think so. I think the American people appreciate somebody bringing up tough issues, particularly when they understand the stakes….

You know, I can't answer your question as to why. I'll continue to do my best. I've tried to make sure the dialogue is elevated. I don't believe I've resorted to name-calling here in Washington, D.C. I find that to not be productive. But I also understand the mind of the American people. They're wondering what's going on. They're wondering why we can't come together and get an energy bill, for example. They're wondering why we can't get Social Security done. And my pledge to the American people is I'll continue to work hard to—with people of both parties and share credit, and give people the benefit of the credit when we get something done.

Apr. 28, 2005

I end this section in true, *officium paci* fashion.

I told all four [of the congressional leaders] that there were going to be some times where we don't agree with each other. But that's okay. If this were a dictatorship, it'd be a heck of a lot easier, just so long as I'm the dictator.

Dec. 18, 2000

I'm a war president. I make decisions here in the Oval Office in foreign-policy matters with war on my mind. Again, I wish it wasn't true, but it is true. And the American people need to know they got a president who sees the world the way it is. And I see dangers that exist, and it's important for us to deal with them.

Meet the Press, Feb. 7, 2004

I wish I wasn't the war president. Who in the heck wants to be a war president? I don't.

Aug. 6, 2004

Bush on Leadership

In the following quotes, Bush explains to the American people why he deserves to be the next president of the United States. I draw here from both campaigns.

In order to be a good president when it comes to foreign policy, it requires someone with vision, judgment, and leadership. I've been the governor of the second biggest state in the United States. If it were a nation, it would be the eleventh largest economy in the world. I was overwhelmingly reelected because the people in my state realized I know how to lead, and I've shown good judgment. A couple of weeks ago, at the Reagan Library, I talked about my vision for peace. My goal, should I become the president, is to keep the peace. I intend to do so by promoting free trade, which, in my judgment, promotes American values across the world. I intend to do so by strengthening alliances, which says America cannot go alone; we must be peacemakers, not peace-

> keepers. And I intend to strengthen the military to make sure that the world is peaceful.
>
> GOP Debate, New Hampshire, Dec. 2, 1999

> Well, I treat people with respect. I don't feel like I'm better than anybody else. I feel like I have the ability to lead. I wouldn't be seeking the presidency if I wasn't confident that I could do the job.
>
> Beliefnet.com, 2000

> I believe I'm going to win, because the American people know I know how to lead. I've shown the American people I know how to lead. I have—I understand everybody in this country doesn't agree with the decisions I've made. And I made some tough decisions. But people know where I stand. People out there listening know what I believe. And that's how best it is to keep the peace.
>
> Bush/Kerry I, Sept. 30, 2004

In an interview in the *Austin American-Statesman*, Bush criticizes Al Gore for being wishy-washy.

> My opponent won't tell you where he stands on this issue. He is afraid to offend somebody, but that's not what a leadership is about. You got to stand strong. If you don't stand for anything, you don't stand for anything. If you don't stand for something, you don't stand for anything.
>
> Nov. 2, 2000

The implication here is that Bush, unlike Gore, stands strong on issues.

From the first Bush/Kerry debate on September 30 of 2004, Bush again "promotes" his own leadership abilities indirectly through his incessant attacks on Senator Kerry.

> First of all, what my opponent wants you to forget is that he voted to authorize the use of force and now says, "It's the *wrong war at the wrong time at the wrong place*". I don't see how you can lead this country to succeed in Iraq if you say, *"Wrong war, wrong time, wrong place"*. What message does that send our troops? What message does that send to our allies? What message does that send the Iraqis?

> My opponent says help is on the way, but what kind of message does it say to our troops in harm's way, "*Wrong war, wrong place, wrong time*"?

> So what's the message going to be: "Please join us in Iraq. We're a grand diversion. Join us for a war that is *the wrong war at the wrong place at the wrong time?*" I know how these people think. I deal with them all the time. I sit down with the world leaders frequently and talk to them on the phone frequently. They're not going to follow somebody who says, *"This is the wrong war at the wrong place at the wrong time"*. They're not going to follow somebody whose core convictions keep changing because of politics in America.
>
> Yes, I understand what it means to the commander in chief. And if I were to ever say, *"This is the wrong war at the wrong time at the wrong place",* the troops would wonder, "How can I follow this guy?" You cannot lead the war on terror if you keep changing positions on the war on terror and say things like, "Well, this is just a grand diversion". It's not a grand diversion. This is an essential that we get it right. And so, the plan he talks about simply won't work.

What is Bush's approach to advancing domestic policies? Decentralization!

> Well, I don't believe in command and control out of Washington, D.C. I believe Washington ought to set standards, but again I think we ought to be collaborative at the local levels and I think we ought to work with people at the local levels.
>
> Bush/Gore II, Oct. 11, 2000

And Bush's foreign policy, prior to 9/11? The second debate with Al Gore is one in which Bush lays out his foreign policy in its most general, humble-but-strong terms.

> I don't think they'll look at us with envy. It really depends upon how our nation conducts itself in foreign policy. *If we're an arrogant nation, they'll resent us. If we're a humble nation, but strong, they'll welcome us.* And it's—*our nation stands alone right now in the world in terms of power, and that's why we have to be humble—and yet project strength in a way that promotes freedom.* So I don't think they ought to look at us in any way other than what we are. *We're a freedom-loving nation and if we're an arrogant nation they'll view us that way, but if we're a humble nation they'll respect us.*

And foreign-policy success, Bush recognized before 9/11, would largely be dictated by Middle East peace.

> I've been a leader. I've been a person who has to set a clear vision and convince people to follow. I've got a strategy for the Middle East. And first let me say that our nation now needs to speak with one voice during this time, and I applaud the president for working hard to diffuse tensions. Our nation needs to be credible and strong. When we say we're somebody's friend, everybody has got to believe it. Israel is our friend and we'll stand by Israel. We need to reach out to modern Arab nations as well. To build coalitions to keep the peace. I also need—the next leader needs to be patient. *We can't put the Middle East peace process on our timetable. It's got to be on the timetable of the people that we're trying to bring to the peace table. We can't dictate the terms of peace,* which means that you have to be steady. You can't worry about polls or focus groups. You've got to have a clear vision. That's what a leader does. A leader also understands that the United States must be strong to keep the peace. Saddam Hussein still is a threat in the Middle East. Our coalition against Saddam is unraveling. Sanctions are loosened. The man who may be developing weapons of mass destruction, we don't know because inspectors aren't in. So to answer your question, it requires a clear vision, a willingness to stand by our friends, and the credibility for people both friend and foe to understand when America says something, we mean it.
>
> Bush/Gore III, Oct. 17, 2000

The humble-but-strong approach, as we have seen, stands in stark contrast to the *officium paci* doctrine adopted after 9/11.

Of course, one key to successful leadership is to make choices autocratically, whenever possible, while leaving people with the illusion that such choices are reflections of their common will.

> My opponent [John Kerry] just said something amazing. He said Osama bin Laden uses the invasion of Iraq as an excuse to spread hatred for America. Osama bin Laden isn't going to determine how we defend ourselves. Osama bin Laden doesn't get to decide. The American people decide. *I decided* [oops!] the right action was in Iraq.
>
> Bush/Kerry I, Sept. 30, 2004

When recently asked if he was troubled by the recent slide in his popularity,[2] Bush replied:

> Polls? You know, if a President tries to govern based upon polls, you're [*sic*] kind of like a dog chasing your tail. I don't think you can make good, sound decisions based upon polls. And I don't think the American people want a President who relies upon polls and focus groups to make decisions for the American people.
>
> Apr. 28, 2005

Of course, polls can give a president a very good idea of where the people stand on a particular issue at any particular time. Does Bush really ignore polls, like he so often says he does? Not a chance!

Finally, Bush was asked at a recent press conference about his administration's policy of paying journalists to promote its agenda.

> Reporter: Mr. President, earlier this year, you told us you wanted your administration to cease and desist on payments to journalists to promote your agenda. You cited the need for ethical concerns and the need for bright line between the press and the government. Your administration continue to make the use of video news releases, which is prepackaged news stories sent to television stations, fully aware that some—or many of these stations will air them without any disclaimer that they are produced by the government. The Comptroller General of the United States, this week, said that raises ethical questions. Does it raise ethical questions about the use of government money to produce stories about the government that wind up being aired with no disclosure that they were produced by the government?
>
> Bush: There is a Justice Department opinion that says these—these pieces are within the law, so long as they're based upon facts, not advocacy. And I expect our agencies to adhere to that ruling, to that Justice Department opinion. This has been a longstanding practice of the federal government to use these types of videos. The Agricultural

---

2 Bush's approval ratings have fallen as low as 40% in late August of 2005 from a high of 52% earlier in the year.

> Department, as I understand it, has been using these videos for a long period of time. The Defense Department, other departments have been doing so. It's important that they be based on the guidelines set out by the Justice Department. Now, I also—I think it would be helpful if local stations, then, disclosed to their viewers that that's—that this was based upon a factual report, and they chose to use it. But evidently, in some cases, that's not the case. So, anyway.
>
> Mar. 16, 2005

On the issue of reform of Social Security, Bush in self-promoting fashion, verbally vaunts of his leadership abilities:

> And so—oh, I know, I've read about so and so, we're not going to talk about this and we're going to throw down this marker. But in the meantime, the people are watching Washington and nothing is happening, except you got a President who's willing to talk about the issue—and a President who, by the way, is going to keep talking about the issue until we get people to the table.
>
> May 31, 2005

Son of "The Wimp"

It's now well known that Bush was deeply distraught about the October 19 of 1987 cover article entitled, "George Bush: Fighting the 'Wimp' Factor", in *Newsweek*. Writes Evan Smith:

> Newsweek reporter, Margaret Warner, wrote the famous "Fighting the Wimp Factor" cover story in October 1987. After it ran, George W. recalled, "Margaret called me on the phone, and I let her have it. I said, 'This is disgraceful. You spent all this time to write a two-page article, and it had the word wimp in it seven times about George Bush?' I was furious. I wasn't yelling, but I was very firm. She blamed it on her editors, and I said, 'Then you ought to quit. You ought to quit if that's the kind of journalistic integrity you have.'" Warner, now the chief Washington correspondent of PBS's *NewsHour with Jim Lehrer,* disputes that account. "I agreed that the use of the word 'wimp' on the cover seemed unnecessarily cruel," she says, "but I had no apologies for

---

3 Evan Smith, "Washington George", *Texas Monthly*, 27 #6, 111-113.

> the story itself. It was a fair look at why Bush had this persistent image problem—that he was, to put it delicately, something less than his own man. The campaign, George W. included, didn't like to admit it.[3]

Daddy's No Wimp

Psychologist Justin A. Frank in *Bush on the Couch* mentions many of the psychological issues that George W. Bush may be fighting: dyslexia, sadism, alcoholism, sense of omnipotence, escapism, inability to grieve, and sense of infallibility.[4] These he traces to Bush's early life—especially his relationship with his seldom-at-home father. Many of the psychological problems the president may be grappling with are attempts, put simply, to prove that he is no wimp. On Bush's use of language, Frank says, "His familiar use of pat phrases and stock expressions suggest that he is compelled to use language less to express than to control; he seeks to manage the message, both by limiting what he says and deflecting others' attempts to engage in dialogue".[5] We shall see many instances of these psychological strategies in the following two chapters.

In this interview below, Bush defends his father from the charge of being a wimp. His ending comments are childlike and perhaps reveal great ambivalence in his relationship to "daddy". That this particular charge should anger him so also shows plainly his own insecurity about his own manhood.

> Beliefnet: I've seen that in the past when you've been asked how people could pray for you, you've said to ask people to pray that God will protect your children because people are going to say ugly and hurtful things about their father during the campaign. What do you mean by that?
>
> Bush: I want them to understand, as best as they can, at the age of 18 years old, what the run for the presidency means, from their perspective. I guess, I hope that intercessory prayers will help ease their mind and calm their fears.

---

4 Justin A. Frank, *Bush on the Couch* (New York: ReganBooks, 2004).

5 Justin A. Frank, *Bush on the Couch,* 123.

Beliefnet:	About what?
Bush:	Well it's about what they hear and, you know, about *people saying ugly things about their daddy. We're a family of love, and I know what it means to have somebody criticize my dad. I didn't like it at all, and it's hurtful.*

Fall 2000, *Beliefnet.com*

Dubya's No Wimp

Bush's own words and actions as governor and president show undue regard for proving to the eyes of the American public and the world that he is no wimp. As governor of Texas, he had put a record number of death-row prisoners to death. As president, he landed on the deck of the USS Abraham Lincoln in a fighter plane on the first of May, 2003, to announce to the world that, for all intents and purposes, the war with Iraq was over. There are numerous other things Bush has said and done that suggest super-compensation toward the Teddy-Roosevelt way of doing things—a super-compensation that masks great insecurity and self-doubt.

Consider, as one illustration, his interview with Diane Sawyer on December 16 of 2003. Throughout the interview, the president's answers to questions are often rudely terse. Many times he answers with a simple "yeah"—as if it is beneath him to be interviewed by a woman. When the topic of the capture of Saddam Hussein comes up, Bush's reply shows no hint at all of compassion. It is blatantly sadistic and Bush focuses on the fact that Hussein was found in a hole, like some rat. After all, "he's the person who tried to kill my dad".[6]

Sawyer:	Would you like to see him [Hussein]?
Bush:	No. I don't care to see him.
Sawyer:	Never?
Bush:	I have no—I've seen him. I've seen enough of him. *I saw him getting de-loused and after having been pulled out a rat hole.*

6 For more on Bush's sadism, see Justin A. Frank, *Bush on the Couch.*

Sawyer: His daughter has said that those photos were disrespectful and humiliating to him. And that he also seemed sedated, by the way.

Bush: Yeah.

Sawyer: Was he sedated? And was it designed to humiliate him?

Bush: No, I don't. First of all, I don't know if he was sedated or not. I mean, that's a question you need to ask the folks in the field. Secondly, *it was designed to reflect the truth and to show, and to show the world that this barbaric person was found in a hole, hiding, cowering, that—it's also interesting that he's going to receive the justice that he never gave others.* And it's, it's a dramatic moment. And I can understand a daughter being concerned about her dad. I mean, there's, you know, presumably somewhere in this hard, barbaric heart, there was some love for his child. And, but he showed no love for the Iraqi people, particularly those that dared express an opinion other than his.

In a press conference the day before the Sawyer interview, Bush replies to other questions about Hussein.

Reporter: Mr. President, good morning. When Saddam emerged from his hole on Saturday, he told a U.S. soldier that he was willing to negotiate. Might there be room for negotiation, perhaps in exchange for a public statement to the Iraqi people that may serve your interest? And, secondly, this soldier also said to Saddam, reportedly, that President Bush sends his greetings. You say this is not personal, but you've also pointed out this was a man who tried to murder your father. What is your greeting to him?

Bush: Good riddance! The world is better off without you, Mr. Saddam Hussein. I find it very interesting that *when the heat got on, you dug yourself a hole and you crawled in it.* And our brave troops, combined with good intelligence, found you. And you'll be brought to justice, something you did not afford the people you brutalized in your own country.

Dec. 16, 2003

These examples illustrate that Bush is fond of "marginalizing" his adversaries. In a press conference earlier in the same year, he referred to Osama bin Ladin as a "parasite" who's "on the run" or "hiding in some cave".

> Well, deep in my heart, I know *the man's on the run if he's alive at all.* And I—you know, *who knows if he's hiding in some cave or not?* We hadn't heard from him in a long time. And the idea of focusing on one person is really—indicates to me people don't understand the scope of the mission. Terror's bigger than one person. And he's just—he's a person *who has now been marginalized.* His network is—his host government has been destroyed. *He's the ultimate parasite who found weakness, exploited it, and met his match.* He is—you know, as I mention in my speeches—I do mention the fact that *this is a fellow who is willing to commit youngsters to their death.* And *he, himself, tries to hide,* if, in fact, he's hiding at all. So I don't know where he is. Nor—you know, I just don't spend that much time on him really, to be honest with you.
>
> March 13, 2002

Here, not just bin Laden, but all terrorists are marginalized.

> This is a war that we fight against these shadowy terrorists that *hide in caves or hide in big cities* and *send young souls to their death through suicide.* That's the kind of people we're after.
>
> July 1, 2002

The very same message about terrorists comes forth in a speech on July 11 of 2005 to the FBI Academy: "This enemy hides in caves and plots in shadows, and then emerges to strike and kill in cold blood in our cities and communities".

In his six years as governor of Texas, Bush executed 152 people—a record for any governor in U.S. history. Regarding his record, he had this to say in the *The Washington Post* on June 22 of 2000: "I analyze each case when it comes across my desk. And as far as I'm concerned, there has not been one innocent person executed since I've been the governor". How can anyone be sure no mistakes were made? Bush gives us his personal assurance and that should be good enough to quiet any critic!

One such instance is the famous case of mass murderer Karla Faye Tucker. After numerous appeals by Tucker to overturn her death sentence, Bush turned to reporter Tucker Carlson, pursed his lips derisively, and mocked the prisoner unsympathetically, "Please don't kill me!"

In the second debate with Gore, Bush shows similar insensitivity to the issue of the death penalty and the deep psychological history of abuse that those who commit such atrocious crimes usually suffer.

> We've got one [hate-crime law] in Texas. *And guess what?* The three men who murdered James Byrd, *guess what's going to happen to them?* They're going to be put to death. A jury found them guilty. It's going to be hard to punish them any worse after they get put to death. And it's the right cause. It's the right decision.
>
> Oct. 11, 2000

The video of the debate betrays clearly a sense of gladness or triumph. One notes that Bush would certainly be in favor of an even greater punishment, if one could be had.

Could the fear of being labeled "wimp" be behind bald statements of machismo such as these?

> All told, more than 3,000 suspected terrorists have been arrested in many countries. Many others have met a different fate. *Let's put it this way—they are no longer a problem to the United States and our friends and allies.*
>
> State of the Union Address, Jan. 28, 2003

> There are some who feel like that, you know, the conditions are such that they [the terrorists] can attack us there. My answer is "*Bring 'em on!*"
>
> Interview with Diane Sawyer, Dec. 16, 2003

> I just remember—all I'm doing is remembering when I was a kid, I remember that—they used to put out there in the old West a "Wanted" poster; it said "*Wanted Dead or Alive*". All I want, and American wants him brought to justice. That's what we want.
>
> Sept. 17, 2001

> In my judgment, when the United States says there will be serious consequences, and if there isn't serious consequences, it creates adverse consequences. People look at us and say, "They don't mean what they say; they are not willing to follow through".
>
> *Meet the Press,* Feb. 7, 2004

Bush's sadism, of course, ties in neatly with his black-and-white thinking about reality. His tendency is to expunge or shut out anything he doesn't quite understand or anything that might turn into a great problem for him. Out of sight; out of mind. And nothing is ever more out of sight than when it's completely exterminated.

All in all, Bush is a president who rides horses and lands fighter planes on ships, not a president who'd ever get caught driving a Mini-Cooper or Bug.

> The folks who conducted to act on our country on September 11th made a big mistake. They underestimated America. They underestimated our resolve, our determination, our love for freedom. They misunderestimated [*sic*] the fact that we love a neighbor in need. They misunderestimated [*sic*] the compassion of our country. I think they misunderestimated [*sic*] the will and determination of the Commander-in-Chief, too.
>
> Sept. 26, 2001

Putting Down Others

Bush is often unabashed about his perception of his own superiority. It's not uncommon for him to parade his superiority by belittling others. Here he unapologetically denigrates a reporter at a White House press conference in the Rose Garden.

> Bush: Let's see. Mark Smith, a radio man.
> Reporter: Thank you very much, sir, for including our radio folks here.
> Bush: A face for radio. (Yucks.)
> Reporter: I wish I could say that was the first time you told me that, sir. (More yucks.)
> Bush: The first time I did it to a national audience, though. (Even more yucks.)
> Reporter: Actually—my wife the last time. (Even more than more yucks.)
>
> Oct. 28, 2003

Immediately after this reporter, another from radio tries to catch the president's ear. Bush shuts the door on him quickly.

Reporter:	Another radio? Another radio, Mr. President?
Bush:	Excuse me—particularly since you interrupted me—no.

About a year and one half later, Bush uses the tired face-for-radio joke at the expense of another reporter trying to do his job.

Bush:	Let's see, have I gone through all the TV personalities yet?
Reporter:	Yes. (Yucks.)
Bush:	Herman.
Reporter:	Mr. President, good morning.
Bush:	A face made for radio, I might add.
Reporter:	Thank you. My mother appreciates it. (Yucks.)

Feb. 17, 2005

While being interviewed in Paris, Bush took to humiliating a reporter.

Reporter:	You said in reaction to demonstrations against you and your administration during this trip in Europe that it's simply a healthy democracy exercising its will, and that disputes are positive. But I wonder why it is you think there are strong—such strong sentiments in Europe against you and against this administration? Why, particularly, there's a view that you and your administration are trying to impose America's will on the rest of the world, particularly when it comes to the Middle East and where the war on terrorism goes next? (Repeated in French) And, Mr. President, would you maybe comment on that?
Bush:	Very good. The guy memorizes four words, and he plays like he's intercontinental. (Yucks.)
Reporter:	I can go on.
Bush:	I'm impressed. Que bueno. Now I'm literate in two languages. (Yucks.)

Paris, May 26, 2002

Why is Bush so condescending to the media? For one, he's got a lot to hide and dissembling through mock displays of power has thus far proven to be an effective defensive mechanism. Secondly, the media clearly intimidates him. One needs merely to note that he only gives press conferences in the U.S.

when he absolutely needs to do so and, when he does, they are usually brief and uninformative.

To protect himself from reporters, Bush has an array of strategies to ward off the press hounds. For instance, in a press conference in Rome with Putin, Bush begins the conference thus:

> With that, I will be glad to answer—both of us will be glad to answer a few questions from you. Let's make your questions short, so that we won't leave my wife waiting at the tarmac in Rome.
>
> July 22, 2001

From his ranch in Crawford with Rumsfeld and Cheney, Bush says:

> Dana, then Mark. We've got to get in before we have a heat stroke. (Yucks!) Before *you* [Cheney] have a heat stroke. (More yucks!)
>
> Crawford, Aug. 8, 2003

Bush ends a press conference from the James Brady Room on March 16 of 2005 in this manner:

> And our diplomatic objective is to continue working with our friends to make it clear to Iran we speak with a single voice.
>
> Listen, whoever thought about modernizing this room deserves a lot of credit. (Yucks!) Like, there's very little oxygen in here anymore. (More yucks!) And so, for the sake of a health press corps and a healthy President, I'm going to end the press conference. But I want to thank you for giving me a chance to come by and visit. I wish you all—genuinely wish you all—a happy Easter holiday with you and your family.

But it is not just to the press that Bush speaks condescendingly. It's his typical manner of speaking to those around him. For example, one of his pet phrases is the paternalistic "good job". At the Focus on Education with President Bush gathering in Springfield, Ohio, Bush speaks to Kathy Rank, teacher of the year.

> You ready to go? Good job. Kathy Rank, sitting right here next to—I'm sitting right here next to the Ohio Teacher of the Year. Thank you.... Yes, good job. That's great. See why she's teacher of the year?

Later, a ninety-nine year old man named Josh gets the good-job treatment: "Good job. Congratulations, Josh. Ninety-nine, brother". Finally, the president gives everyone one final "good job" toward the end of the event.

> Great. Good job. Thanks for coming. Listen, thank you all for being here. We're making progress. We're achieving what every American wants, every child receive—being able to realize their dreams through a good education.
>
> Sept. 27, 2004

The "good job" pet phrase may not seem so repugnant when used at rallies for education, like above, but Bush somctimcs speaks thus to foreign dignitaries. Here it is entirely out of place. In a joint press conference with President Allawi of Iraq on September 23 of 2004, Bush ends: "Mr. Prime Minister, appreciate you. Good job". At another press conference with newly elected President Abbas of Palestine, after the later gave a short address in Washington on May 26 of 2005, Bush stated: "Good job. Good job. Two questions a side, starting with Terry".

Bush's Dyslexia

Is Bush dyslexic? Consider a brief exchange with Larry King on September 29 of 2000 about Gail Sheehy's article in *Vanity Fair* that proposed Bush had dyslexia.

King:	So how did you react when a thing like that made—
Bush:	I just smiled. Just thought it was silly, you know. We've got a writer who just made something up. And, you know, I'm—even if I were, I would be a good president. But I'm not.

The adding of “But I’m not” after the counterfactual conditional, “If I were, I would…”, suggests Bush is confusing a counterfactual conditional with an ordinary conditional. The counterfactual force of “If I were” implies “I am not”.

Diane Sawyer brought up Bush’s dislike of reading in her interview with Bush. The president, after a couple of condescending “yeahs”, replies as follows:

Sawyer: First of all, I just want to ask about reading. And, Mr. President, you know that there was a great deal of reporting about the fact that you said, first of all, that you let Condoleezza Rice and Andrew Card give you a flavor of what’s in the news.
Bush: Yeah.
Sawyer: That you don’t read the stories yourself.
Bush: Yeah. I get my news from people who don’t editorialize. *They give me the actual news.* And it makes it easier to digest, on a daily basis, *the facts.*
Sawyer: Is it just harder to read constant criticism or to read?
Bush: Why even put up with it when you can get the facts elsewhere? I’m a lucky man. I’ve got, it’s not just Condi and Andy. It’s all kinds of people in my Administration who are charged with different responsibilities. And they come in and say, “This is what’s happening. This isn’t what’s happening”.
Sawyer: You don’t think you’re missing anything by not reading?
Bush: *Missing opinion.*

Bush is frank in an interview with Brit Hume about his getting the daily news from his staff, instead of reading for himself.

Hume: How do you get your news?
Bush: I get briefed by Andy Card and Condi in the morning. They come in and tell me. In all due respect, you’ve got a beautiful face and everything. I glance at the headlines just to kind of a flavor for what’s moving. I rarely read the stories, and get briefed by people who are probably read the news themselves. But like Condoleezza, in her case, the national security adviser is getting her news directly from the participants on the world stage.

Hume: Has that been your practice since day one, or is that a practice that you've—

Bush: Practice since day one.

Hume: Really?

Bush: Yes. You know, look, I have great respect for the media. I mean, our society is a good, solid democracy because of a good, solid media. But I also understand that a lot of times there's opinions mixed in with news. And I—

Hume: I won't disagree with that, sir.

Bush: I appreciate people's opinions, but I' more interested in news. And the best way to get the news is from objective sources. And *the most objective sources I have are people on my staff* who tell me what's happening in the world.

Sept. 22, 2003

Two comments are in order here. First, it's rather astonishing that a president, who sets a high priority on reading (NCLB), has himself distaste for reading. Secondly, Bush's staff is known for its blend of right-wing nationalists and neo-conservatives—an unlikely blend to give one an objective slant on current events.

Surprisingly, Bush in the last couple of years has taken to flaunting publicly his fondness of reading—especially when it comes to history. Was he fooling everyone all along? It's unlikely. What's more likely is that this recent flaunting of his passion for history is a rather meager and unconvincingly attempt to change his dumb-guy image. In an interview aboard Air Force One, en route to Texas, Bush said:

> Like Stretch, I'm on the injured reserve list from running, so I'll be mountain biking. I think Cat McKinnon is going come up from Austin. Oh, yes. And I'll be fishing. I'll be finishing my book, *Peter the Great,* by Robert K. Massey. Some of you old-timers have probably already read it, I'm just now—have you read it?
>
> Apr. 8, 2005

Finally, in an interview at the White House by a member of the Danish Broadcasting Corporation, Bush, in an unconvincing manner, answers a question given by the reporter's daughter about what he does in his spare time.

> I read a lot. And so when I—tell your daughter—right before I go to bed, after I do my homework. I'm an avid reader. I like to read history. I just finished a book about George Washington. And so I get my mind off my work, and get my—I get—if I've got troubles, I get my—get the troubles off my mind by reading a lot. And then I—I'm kind of getting to be an old guy, so I fall asleep about 9:30 p.m., much to the chagrin of Laura Bush. Up at 5:15 a.m., I get to work about 6:45 a.m.
>
> June 29, 2005

Bush's Substance Abuse

When it comes to his use of alcohol and other drugs, Bush has consistently lied, dissimulated, or refused to answer any and all such questions—very uncharacteristic of one for whom accountability is so important.

When confronted with his past use of substances, in some such cases, he employs a three point strategy. First, he states that *it's not important to revisit the past*. Second, he adds that what is important is—and here is moral point one—that *he has learned from his mistakes*. Third, if pushed further about revisiting the past, he sometimes states—and here is moral point two—that *his revisiting the past could send bad signals to others to try alcohol (or drugs)*. For instance, in reply to a question from Steve Cooper about whether he ever used drugs, Bush stated:

> (1) *I'm not going to talk about what I did as a child* [*sic*]. What I'm going to talk about, and I'm going to say this consistently: (1) *It is irrelevant what I did twenty to thirty years ago.* (2) *What's relevant is that I have learned from any mistakes that I made.* (3) *I do not want to send signals to anybody that what Governor Bush did thirty years ago is cool to try.*

In an interview with Tim Russert some nine months later, he uses exactly the same three-point strategy to answer a similar question.

> (1) *I've said all I'm going to say about what I may or may not have done.* Here's the important thing that I think baby-boomer generations ought

> to be saying: (2) *If we've made mistakes, we've learned from our mistakes; if we made mistakes when we were young, that we've learned and we're responsible citizens.* And we're willing to say to children, who are listening to words that people like me utter, "Don't use drugs". (3) *I don't want to provide any excuse, Tim, for your fourteen-year-old child to say, "Hey, maybe is old Governor Bush did something, I think I'm going to try it, Dad".* That's irresponsible behavior.
>
> *Meet the Press*, Nov. 21, 1999

Finally, according to J. H. Hatfield in *Fortunate Son*, when Bush was busted for cocaine in 1972 in Houston, his father got him off the hook on the slight condition that George W. perform several months of community service at Project PULL—a non-profit organization for troubled youths. On December 16 of 1999, Larry King addressed the issue of hypocrisy—that others have gone to prison for the same crime, while Bush, because of his father's impact, has escaped serious punishment. Bush stubbornly refused to talk about "his past" with King. When King asked why Bush wasn't troubled by the hypocrisy, Bush ended the conversation thus:

> Here's what people need to know about me: that *I'm going to bring honor and dignity*, that *I've learned from mistakes made*, that *I am prepared to send a message of personal responsibility*, and that's what I'm going to do.
>
> *Larry King Live*, CNN, Dec. 16, 1999

The blatant hypocrisy behind this answer needs no comment.

The "Compassionate Conservative"

The year 2002 was the year Bush showcased his "Compassionate Conservatism". Addresses this year were filled with the two words or variations of them.

> We've got pockets of persistent poverty in our society, which I refuse to declare defeat—I mean, I refuse to allow them to continue on. And so one of the things that we're trying to do is to encourage a faith-based ini-

tiative to spread its wings all across America, to be able to capture this great compassionate spirit.

O'Fallon, MO, Mar. 18, 2002

In a speech in Cleveland at the Playhouse Square Center, Bush explained just what "compassionate conservatism" was.

Our aim isn't to make government bigger by spending more money; our aim isn't to focus on finance, large or small. Our aim must be to mean that *when we spend money, we spend it on what works to create a better society.* I call this compassionate conservatism.

It is *conservative* to trust the local folks to chart the path to excellence in education. It's *conservative* to liberate parents. It's *conservative* to pass power out of Washington, D.C. when it comes to public schools. It is *compassionate* to make sure not one child gets left behind in America. It is *conservative* to promote private property, and ownership of homes.

It is *compassionate* to understand there is an ownership gap in America, and we must use our resources to close that ownership gap by encouraging minority ownership of homes in America.

It's *conservative* to reform welfare and reduce dependence on government.

It is *compassionate* to encourage work and family and values of personal responsibility.

It is *conservative* to understand government can hand out money, but it cannot put hope in people's hearts and, therefore, we should promote the good works of faith-based and community-based programs.

It is *compassionate* to understand in the land of plenty there are pockets of despair and hopelessness.

There are people who, when you say the American Dream, say, I don't know what that means. And it's *compassionate* to understand all of us, no matter what your political party is, must do something about it. We must work to make the American Dream reach into every single neighborhood all across America.

July 1, 2002

Some months later, he would add:

The goals for this country are peace in the world. And the goals for this country are a compassionate American for every single citizen. That compassion is found in the hearts and souls of the American citizens.

Dec. 19, 2002

Again, in an address in West Virginia:

> I want—I'm going to Nashville tomorrow to talk about the compassion agenda. We've got a role in Washington, but the biggest role, of course, takes place in the neighborhoods of our country, when people hear the call to love somebody like they'd like to be loved themselves; when people fully understand that one person can make a significant difference in the life of somebody who hurts.
>
> Feb. 9, 2003

In a press conference on May 31 of 2005, Bush speaks about his administrations' desire, through compassion, to help the "least of us" in America.

> Well, part of it, Jonathan, is just to—is to constantly remind people that we have a responsibility to the less—to the least of us in our society. I mean, part of a culture of life is to continue to expand the faith-based and community-based initiative to help people who hurt. Part of it is to recognize that in a society that is as blessed as we are that we have a responsibility to help others, such as AIDS victims on the continent of Africa, or people who hunger in sub-Sahara, for example. So the culture of life is more than just an issue like embryonic stem cell; it's promoting a culture that is mindful that we can help—to help save lives through compassion. And my administration will continue to do so.

Finally, in an address at the Indiana Black Exposition in Indianapolis on July 14 of 2005, Bush upped the compassionate conservative rhetoric a notch.

> I see an America where all our children are taught the basic skills they need to live up to their God-given potential. I see an America where every citizen owns a stake in the future of our country, and where a growing economy creates jobs and opportunity for everyone. I see an America where most troubled neighborhoods become safe places of kinship and community. I see an America where every person of every race has the opportunity to strive for a better future and to take part of the promise of America. That's what I see. And I believe the government has a role to play in helping people gain the tools they need to build lives of dignity and purpose. That's at the heart of what I call compassionate conservatism.

Bush, of course, cannot be describing the current state of affairs in America. Nor can he be describing a state of affairs is possible with his domestic agenda. What then, we may ask, does he really see?

The Uniter

Bush's boasts that he was one to unify the American people and the U.S. congress was never more evident as it was when he stormed on the scene in his candidacy for the presidency in 2000. Consider the first Bush/Gore debate of October 3 of 2000.

> And I've been the chief executive officer of the second biggest state in the union. I have *a proud record of working with both Republicans and Democrats*, which is what our nation needs.
>
> Now, they may blame other folks, but it's time to get somebody in Washington who is going *to work with both Republicans and Democrats* to get some positive things done when it comes to our seniors.
>
> Same with Social Security. I think there was a good opportunity *to bring Republicans and Democrats together* to reform the Social Security system so seniors will never go without.
>
> *I'm going to work with Democrats and Republicans to reform the system.*
>
> I've been the governor of a big state. I think one of the hallmarks of my relationship in Austin, Texas, is that I've had *the capacity to work with both Republicans and Democrats.* I think that's an important part of leadership. I think what it means to build consensus. I've shown I know how to do so. Tonight in the audience there's one elected state senator who is a Democrat, a former state-wide officer who is a Democrat, a lot of Democrats who are here in the debate to—because they want to show their support that shows I know how to lead.
>
> Testing is the cornerstone of reform. You know how I know? Because it's the cornerstone of reform in the State of Texas. *Republicans and*

Democrats came together and said what can we do to make our public education the best in the country?

In his third debate with John Kerry in 2004, Bush promised to bring the two parties together on the issue of Social Security reform.

> But for our children and our grandchildren, we need to have a different strategy [for Social Security]. And recognizing that, I called together a group of our fellow citizens to study the issue. It was a committee chaired by the late Senator Daniel Patrick Moynihan of New York, *a Democrat.* And they came up with a variety of ideas for people to look at. I believe that younger workers ought to be allowed to take some of their own money and put it in a personal savings account, because I understand that they need to get better rates of return than the rates of return being given in the current Social Security trust. And the compounding rate of interest effect will make it more likely that the Social Security system is solvent for our children and our grandchildren. *I will work with Republicans and Democrats.* It'll be a vital issue in my second term. It is an issue that I am willing to take on, *and so I'll bring Republicans and Democrats together.*

He would add later:

> My biggest disappointment in Washington is how partisan the town is. *I had a record of working with Republicans and Democrats as the governor of Texas,* and I was hopeful I'd be able to do the same thing. And we made good progress early on. The No Child Left Behind Act, incredibly enough, was good work between me and my administration and people like Senator Ted Kennedy. And we worked together with Democrats to relieve the tax burden on the middle class and all who pay taxes in order to make sure this economy continues to grow. But Washington is a tough town. And the way I view it is there's a lot of entrenched special interests there, people who are, you know, on one side of the issue or another and they spend enormous sums of money and they convince different senators to taut their way or different congressmen to talk about their issue, and they dig in. I'll continue, in the four years, to continue to try to work to do so. My opponent said this is a bitterly divided time. Pretty divided in the 2000 election. *So in other words, it's pretty divided during the 1990s as well.*
>
> Bush/Kerry III, Oct. 13, 2004

How Bush is able to conclude from all of this that it was "pretty divided during the 1990s as well" is anyone's guess.

Why is it that many people consider Bush to be a divider, when he's been boasting for years about his capacity to bring "Democrats and Republicans together"?

Russert: Tom Daschle, the Democratic Leader in the Senate, said that you've changed the tone for the worse; that it's more acrimonious, more confrontations, that you are the most partisan political president he's ever worked with. Our exit polls of primary voters, not just Democrats but Independents in South Carolina and New Hampshire, more than 70 percent of them said they are angry or dissatisfied with you, and they point to this whole idea of being a uniter as opposed to a divider. Why do you think you are perceived as such a divider?

Bush: *Gosh, I don't know, because I'm working hard to unite the country.* As a matter of fact, it's the hardest part of being the president. I was successful as the governor of Texas for bringing people together for the common good, and I must tell you it's tough here in Washington, and frankly it's the biggest disappointment that I've had so far of coming to Washington.

I'm not blaming anybody. *It's just the environment here is such that it is difficult to find common ground....*

And—but I will continue to work hard to unite the country....

Russert: But around the world, in Europe, favorable ratings—unfavorable ratings, 70 in Germany, 67 in France.

Bush: But you know, Tim, that—

Russert: Why do people hold you in such low esteem?

Bush: *Heck, I don't know*, Ronald Reagan was unpopular in Europe when he was President, according to Jose Maria Aznar. And I said, "You know something?" He said to me, he said, "You're nearly as unpopular as Ronald Reagan was". I said, "So, first of all, I'm keeping pretty good company".

I think that people—when you do hard things, when you ask hard things of people, it can create tensions. And I—heck, I don't know why people do it. I'll tell you, though, I'm not going to change, see? I'm not trying to accommodate—I won't change my philosophy or my point of view. I believe I owe it to the American people to

> say what I'm going to do and do it, and to speak as clearly as I can, try to articulate as best I can why I make decisions I make, but I'm not going to change because of polls. That's just not my nature.
>
> *Meet the Press*, Feb. 7, 2004

Finally, in a recent address to the American public, Bush vaunted of his ability to bring both parties together to pass the No Child Left Behind Act.

> The system for too long had just shuffled children through and just hoped for the best. And guess what happened? We had people graduating from high school who were illiterate—and that's just not right in America. It wasn't working. And so I came to Washington and worked with both Republicans and Democrats—this is a case where bipartisanship was really working well.
>
> Apr. 28, 2005

The Progressivist

Being president of the United States is an extraordinarily challenging job, to say the least. People always expect results and results are often not forthcoming. When they are coming, they might not be coming quickly enough. And so, Bush has quickly come to learn that the role of a president is to instill optimism in people, whether it can be grounded in reality or not.

Since becoming president, Bush has made it a habit to say on every occasion that his administration is "making progress" on any issue that comes up—especially on the war in Iraq, where progress is almost impossible to define or gauge. Consider below the progress being made on every issue imaginable in a press conference on April 28 of 2005.

On reform of Social Security:

> I've also spent time assuring seniors they'll get their [Social Security] check. That's a very important part of making sure we end up with a Social Security reform. I think if seniors feel like they're not going to

get their check, obviously nothing is going to happen. *And we're making progress there, too, Terry, as well.*

On insurgency and democratic reforms in Iraq:

Reporter: Your top military officer, General Richard Myers, says the Iraqi insurgency is as strong now as it was a year ago. Why is that the case? And why haven't we been more successful in limiting the violence?

Bush: I think he went on to say we're winning, if I recall. But nevertheless, there are still some in Iraq who aren't happy with democracy. They want to go back to the old days of tyranny and darkness, torture chambers and mass graves. I believe *we're making really good progress* in Iraq, because the Iraqi people are beginning to see the benefits of a free society....

I also want to caution you all that it's not easy to go from a tyranny to a democracy. We didn't pass sovereignty but about 10 months ago, and since that time *a lot of progress has been made* and *we'll continue to make progress* for the good of the region and for the good of our country.

But our strategy is to stay on the offense, is to keep the pressure on these people, is to cut off their money and to share intelligence and to find them where they hide. And *we are making good progress.*

In the long run, Terry—like I said earlier—the way to defeat terror, though, is to spread freedom and democracy. It's really the only way in the long-term. In the short-term, we'll use our troops and assets and agents to find these people and to protect America. But in the long-term, we must defeat the hopelessness that allows them to recruit by spreading freedom and democracy. But *we're making progress.*

Thirdly, a fundamental problem has been whether or not there's an established chain of command, whether or not a civilian government can say to the military, here's what you need to do—and whether the command goes from top to bottom and the plans get executed. And General Petreaus was telling me *he's pleased with the progress being made* with setting up a command structure, but there's still more work to be done.

One of the real dangers, David, is that as politics takes hold in Iraq, whether or not the civilian government will keep intact the military structure that we're now helping them develop. And my message to the Prime Minister and our message throughout government to the Iraqis is, keep stability; don't disrupt the training that has gone on—don't politicize your military—in other words, have them there to help secure the people.

So *we're making good progress.* We've reduced our troops from 160,000 more or less to 139,000. As you know, I announced to the country that we would step up our deployments—step up deployments and retain some troops for the elections. And then I said we'd get them out, and we've done that. In other words, the withdrawals that I said would happen, have happened.

On the budget:

There's a budget agreement, and I'm grateful for that. In other words, *we are making progress.*

On education:

Yes, I think it's [No Child Left Behind] working. And the reason why I think it's working is because we're measuring, and *the measurement is showing progress toward teaching people how to read and write* and add and subtract. Listen, the whole theory behind No Child Left Behind is this: if we're going to spend federal money, we expect the states to show us whether or not we're achieving simple objectives—like literacy, literacy in math, the ability to read and write. And, yes, *we're making progress.* And I can say that with certainty because we're measuring, Richard.

Apr. 28, 2005

Consider next this exchange between Tim Russert and Bush in a 2004 interview on *Meet the Press.*

Bush: If I could share some stories with you about some of the people I have seen from Iraq, the leaders from Iraq, there is no question in my mind that people that I have seen at least are thrilled with the activities we've taken. There is a nervousness [*sic*] about their future, however.

Russert: If the Iraqi people choose—

Bush: Well, let me finish on the nervousness. I don't want to leave it on that note. There's nervousness because they're not exactly sure what their form of government will look like, and there is—you can understand why. In nine

> months' time, there's—we're now saying, democracy must flourish. And as I recall from my history, it took us quite a while here in the United States, but nevertheless *we are making progress*.
>
> Feb. 7, 2004

I close this section and this chapter with some of Bush's closing sentiments in the second debate with Kerry.

> The great contest for the presidency is about the future, who can lead, who can get things done. We've been through a lot together as a country—been through a recession, corporate scandals, war. *And yet think about where we are:* Added 1.9 million new jobs over the past 13 months. The farm income in America is high. Small businesses are flourishing. Homeownership rate is at an all-time high in America. *We're on the move.*
>
> Oct. 8, 2004

With the state of the nation at the time and the senseless violence in Iraq, the false sense of optimism here is almost morally abhorrent. One wonders either about the president's motives or his grasp of reality.

PART TWO
THROUGH THE LOOKING GLASS

Section Three
Bush's Use of Rhetorical Devices

> "[T]hat's just the nature of democracy. Sometimes pure politics enters into the rhetoric".
>
> George W. Bush

As the previous chapters have shown, George W. Bush is an invidious person and a most unscrupulous president. The following instances will suffice as illustrations:

- Prior to becoming president, he warned against the use of U.S. troops in foreign lands; after becoming president, he rushed forth and attacked Iraq by misleading Congress and the public on WMDs;
- He preaches accountability—even flew in a plane dubbed *Accountability One*—but refuses to hold himself accountable for anything he has done as president;
- He states flatly that we have a duty to promote global peace, but he advocates military measures to achieve such a peace;
- He encourages children to read so that they might attain their goals, although he got where his is through being his father's son and he himself hates to read;
- He promotes himself by putting down others;

- As a "compassionate conservative", he encourages compassion, although he sends hundreds of thousands of troops to fight an unjust war and pays little heed to the many thousands of incidental casualties in Afghanistan and Iraq;
- He maintains that he is as concerned as anyone about the environment, but he refuses any solution that would entail a slowing of American economic prosperity;
- He preaches government by the people, but practices politics as an autocrat, who needs to answer to no one; and
- He asserts that moral values are absolute, but is never at a loss to justify any of his decisions by the present "progress" the U.S. is making or some imagined future, where a situation that now seems dire or chaotic will be stable and prosperous.

In this chapter, I ask a question asked by David Corn in *The Lies of George W. Bush:* "How does he get away with it (so far)?"[1] A good part of the answer—and Corn makes a good case for this—is that he lies. Yet a complete answer is more subtle than this. First, as we saw in the previous chapter, Bush, more than any other president in recent history, avoids the press as much as his office will allow. Second and more to the point of the following chapers in this section. Bush is a sophist—in the traditional sense of the word. He employs, both consciously and unconsciously, an array of rhetorical devices that function both to reinforce the notion that he has duty to promote global peace (the *officium paci* doctrine)—perhaps even at the behest of God—and, at the same time, to buffer him from the dangers of reality that challenge this delusion. If Freud can he used as an authority here, Bush is trading in neurotic currency:

---

[1] David Corn. *The Lies of George W. Busy: Mastering the Politics of Deception* (New York: Three Rivers Press, 2003), 309

> Neurotics live in a world apart, where, as I have said elsewhere, only "neurotic currency" is legal tender; that is to say, they are only affected by what is thought with intensity and pictured with emotion, whereas agreement with external reality is a matter of no importance.[2]

In follows, I summarize Bush's use of rhetorical devices by subsuming them under four simple rules. Many of these rhetorical devices, it will be obvious, are fallacious forms of reasoning. In logic, a *fallacy* or fallacious argument is a mistake in reasoning whereby the reasons given on behalf of some claim (the premises) fail to give sufficient support for that claim (the conclusion). Fallacies are very common in political rhetoric, as a substantial amount of it is propagandist and not evidentially based, but they seem to be more common out of the mouth of Bush. This section then is a closer look at the "logic" of George W. Bush.

---

2 Sigmund Freud, *Totem and Taboo*, trans. James Strachey (New York: W. W. Norton & Company, 1989), 108.

Chapter Six
Rule I: Keep Your "Adversary" Off-Guard

"'...the twinkling of the tea—'
"'The twinkling of what?*' said the [Red] King.*
"'It began with the tea', the Hatter replied.
"'Of course twinkling begins with a T!' said the King sharply. 'Do you take me for a dunce? Go on!'"

To all intents and purposes here, for Bush the term "adversary" may be understood as one who does not trade with the same psychological currency as does he—that is, one who does not share in his same delusional, black-and-white perception of global events. If this is not too far off mark, then almost everyone in the world—outside of his advisors, the radically right nationalists and neoconservatives, and Rush Limbaugh and his Limbaughites—qualifies as an adversary. Almost everyone in the world, then, is a potential threat to his delusions.

How, then, does Bush function and cope with such omnipresent threats? It's reasonable to assert that he must have coping strategies, both conscious and unconscious, and plenty of them. In this chapter, I focus on aggressive coping strategies as a means of keeping one's "adversary" off-guard.

Appeals to Fear

One of the most common aggressive rhetorical devices used by Bush is the appeal to fear. The appeal to fear was not only the mechanism for his reelection; it was also the mechanism for initiating the war with Iraq and sustaining support for it.

In the following passage, Bush appeals to fear in an effort to gather support for war with Iraq.

> Failure to act would embolden other tyrants, allow terrorists access to new weapons and new resources, and make blackmail a permanent feature of world events. The United Nations would betray the purpose of its founding, and prove irrelevant to the problems of our time. And through its inaction, *the United States would resign itself to a future of fear.* That is not the America I know. That is not the America I serve. *We refuse to live in fear.* This nation, in world war and in Cold War, has never permitted the brutal and lawless to set history's course. Now, as before, we will secure our nation, protect our freedom, and help others to find freedom of their own.
>
> Cincinnati, Oct. 7, 2002

Consider also the "lessons of September the 11th".

> We must never forget the lessons of September the 11th. The terrorists will strike, and they will kill innocent life, not only in front of a Red Cross headquarters, they will strike and kill in America, too.
>
> Oct. 27, 2003

Next, there is Bush's opening salvo in his third debate with Kerry. It is a justification for Bush's aggressive military crusade by an appeal to fear. Notice how often he appeals to American safety and security.

> Thank you very much. I want to thank Arizona State as well. Yes, *we can be safe and secure, if we stay on the offense against the terrorists and if we spread freedom and liberty around the world.* I have got a comprehensive strategy to not only chase down the Al Qaida, wherever it exists—and we're making progress; three-quarters of Al Qaida leaders have been brought to justice—but to make sure that countries that har-

bor terrorists are held to account. As a result of securing ourselves and ridding the Taliban out of Afghanistan, the Afghan people had elections this weekend. And the first voter was a 19-year-old woman. Think about that. Freedom is on the march. We held to account a terrorist regime in Saddam Hussein. In other words, *in order to make sure we're secure,* there must be a comprehensive plan. My opponent just this weekend talked about how terrorism could be reduced to a nuisance, comparing it to prostitution, illegal gambling. *I think that attitude and that point of view is dangerous. I don't think you can secure America for the long run* if you don't have a comprehensive view as to how to defeat these people. At home, *we'll do everything we can to protect the homeland.* I signed the homeland security bill to better align our assets and resources. My opponent voted against it. *We're doing everything we can to protect our borders and ports.* But *absolutely we can be secure in the long run.* It just takes good, strong leadership

Oct. 13, 2004

In an interview from Crawford with Egyptian President Hosni Mubarek, Bush says that terrorism is a threat to "all of us".

We recognize that the starting point for a prosperous and peaceful Middle East must be the rejection of terror. Egypt has taken a firm stand against terror by working to disrupt the activities and capabilities of the region's terrorist organizations. These are the policies of a nation and a statesman that understand *the threat that terrorism poses to all of us—to my nation, to his, to all the Arab states, to Israel and to the future of any Palestinian state.* Terrorism must be opposed and it must be defeated. And I'm grateful for President Mubarek's support in the global war against terror.

Apr. 12, 2004

In a press conference in April of 2005, Bush states we must not relax and think that no other terrorist acts will occur in the United States.

One of my—I've said this before to you, I'm going to say it again — one of my concerns after September the 11th is the farther away we got from September the 11th, the more relaxed we would all become and assume that there wasn't an enemy out there ready to hit us. And *I just can't let the American people—I'm not going to let them down by assuming that*

> *the enemy is not going to hit us again.* We're going to do everything we can to protect us. And we've got guidelines. We've got law. But you bet, Mark, we're going to find people before they harm us.
>
> Apr. 28, 2005

Striking Back

A second rhetorical device for keeping adversaries off-guard is to strike back decisively after one is struck first. For instance, prior to becoming president, journalist Andy Hiller of WHDH in Boston caught Bush off-guard when he asked the candidate whether he could name the leaders of Chechnya, Taiwan, Pakistan, and India. Bush failed on the first three and, upon giving up on the last, turned the tables on Hiller.

> Bush: The new prime minister of India is—no. Can *you* name the foreign minister of Mexico?
>
> Hiller: No, sir. No, sir. But I would say to that, I'm not running for president.
>
> Bush: I understand. I understand, but the point I say to you is—is that you know—if what you're suggesting is—is that—what I'm suggesting to you is if you can't name the foreign minister of Mexico, therefore—you know—you're not capable of what you do. But the truth of the matter is—you're is—you are, whether you can or not.
>
> Nov. 4, 1999

It was a victory for Bush, insofar as he always considers any escape from a tough situation to be a victory, but it was as Pyrrhic a victory as his reply was incomprehensible.

When Gore continued to push on the theme that Bush's proposed tax cut would favor mightily the top one percent, Bush shot back quickly and falsely in their third debate by attacking Gore's plan.

> Bush: Fifty million Americans get no tax relief under *his* plan.
>
> Gore: That's not right!

Bush: You may not be one of them, you're just not one of the right people. And secondly, we've had enough fighting. It's time to unite. You talk about eight years? In eight years they haven't gotten anything done on Medicare, on Social Security, a patient's bill of rights. It's time to get something done!

Oct. 17, 2000

Striking First

Bush is savvy enough, at times, to recognize present and certain danger and one of the mechanisms he's adopted to cope with such situations is that of landing the first blow. Consider the number of times he accused Gore of trying to scare people to vote for him—a childish and insubstantive rhetorical device that Bush worked to perfection in his second run for president in 2000 (on account of 9/11).

> I guess my answer to that is the man is running on *Medi-scare*—trying to *frighten* people into the voting booth.
>
> I cannot let this go by, the old-style Washington politics, if we're going to *scare* you in the voting booth.
>
> Look, this is a man who has great numbers. He talks about numbers. I'm beginning to think not only did he invent the Internet, but he invented the calculator. It's fuzzy math. It's a *scaring*—he's trying to *scare* people in the voting booth.
>
> For those of you who *[sic]* he wants to *scare* into the voting booth to vote for him, hear me loud and clear. A promise made will be a promise kept.
>
> Bush/Gore I, Oct. 3, 2000

Bush adopted a similar strategy in his debates with Kerry, four years later. Here the attack was based on Kerry's avowed "inconsistency".

The only consistent about my opponent's position is that he's been inconsistent. He changes positions. And *you cannot change positions in this war on terror if you expect to win.* And I expect to win. It's necessary we win. We're being challenged like never before. And we have a duty to our country and to future generations of America to achieve a free Iraq, a free Afghanistan, and to rid the world of weapons of mass destruction.

Bush/Kerry I, Sept. 30, 2004

I can see why people at your workplace think he changes positions a lot, because he does. He said he voted for the $87 billion, and voted against it right before he voted for it. And that sends a confusing signal to people. He said he thought Saddam Hussein was a grave threat, and now he said it was a mistake to remove Saddam Hussein from power. No, *I can see why people think that he changes position quite often, because he does.* You know, for a while he was a strong supporter of getting rid of Saddam Hussein. He saw the wisdom—until the Democrat primary came along and Howard Dean, the anti-war candidate, began to gain on him, and *he changed positions.* I don't see how you can lead this country in a time of war, in a time of uncertainty, *if you change your mind because of politics....* It's—you've got to be consistent when you're the president. There's a lot [*sic*] of pressures. And you've got to be firm and consistent.

Bush/Kerry II, Oct. 8, 2004

In an interview on Air Force One, Bush used the magic-wand argument to keep an interviewer off-guard.

> Listen, the energy bill is certainly no quick fix. You can't wave a *magic wand.* I wish I could. It's like that soldier at Fort Hood that said, "How come you're not lowering the price of gasoline?" I was having lunch with the fellow, and he said, "Go lower the price of gasoline, President". I said, "I wish I could". It just doesn't work that way.

Apr. 28, 2005

Bulldozing

Bulldozing is a rhetorical technique whereby one goes forward aggressively with what one is asserting regardless of whether what one is asserting is sensible or inane. Consider this exchange between Bush and Gore in their third debate. Gore, accused by Bush of proposing the largest spending in years, has just defended himself by reference to the Clinton-Gore spending record of the last four years.

Lehrer:	Governor, the vice president says you're wrong.
Bush:	*Well, he's wrong. Just add up all the numbers. It's three times bigger than what President Clinton proposed. The Senate Budget Committee—*
Lehrer:	Three times—excuse me, three times bigger than what President Clinton proposed?
Gore:	That was in an ad, Jim, that was knocked down by the journalists who analyzed the ad and said it was misleading.
Bush:	*My turn?*
Lehrer:	Yes, sir.
Bush:	*Forget the journalists. He proposed more than Walter Mondale and Michael Dukakis combined. This is a big spender. And you ought to be proud of it—it's part of his record.* We just have a different philosophy.

Bush/Gore III, Oct. 17, 2000

Note here the path Bush takes. First, he makes an exorbitant claim "It's three times bigger than what President Clinton proposed" that cannot be substantiated. Second, when challenged on the claim, he merely sloughs off the criticism: "Forget the journalists". Third, he plows ahead with another, perhaps equally dubious claim, "He proposed more than Walter Mondale and Michael Dukakis combined". Next comes the conclusion: "This is a big spender". Finally, there's closure: "We just have a different philosophy". At each step, Bush bulldozes ahead, regardless of what is put before him, and puts a cap on things—thereby making it difficult to respond.

The following exchange with Diane Sawyer is another example of a bullying Bush, intent on refusing to consider the possibility of having made a mistake in invading Iraq. I quote at length.

Sawyer:	And now, those controversial Administration statements leading America to war. Their own chief weapons inspector, David Kay, has not found weapons of mass destruction. Fifty percent of the American people have said that

they think the Administration exaggerated the evidence going into the war with Iraq, weapons of mass destruction, connection to terrorism. Are the American people wrong, misguided?

Bush: No, the intelligence I operated on was good sound intelligence. The same intelligence that my predecessor operated on. The—there is no doubt that Saddam Hussein was a threat. The—otherwise the United Nations wouldn't have passed, you know, resolution after resolution after resolution demanding that he disarm. I first went to the United Nations, September the 12th, 2002, and said, "You've given this man resolution after resolution after resolution. He's ignoring them. You step up and see that he honor those resolutions. Otherwise, you become a feckless, debating society". And so, for the sake of peace and for the sake of freedom of the Iraqi people, for the sake of the security of the country, and for the sake of the credibility of international institutions, a group of us moved. And *the world is better for it.*

Sawyer: When you take a look back, Vice President Cheney said, "There is no doubt Saddam Hussein has weapons of mass destruction". Not programs, not intent. There is no doubt he has weapons of mass destruction. Secretary Powell said "100 to 500 tons of chemical weapons". And now the inspectors say that there's no evidence of these weapons existing right now. The yellow cake in Niger. George Tenet has said that shouldn't have been in your speech. Secretary Powell talked about mobile labs. Again, the intelligence, the inspectors have said they can't confirm this, they can't corroborate. Nuclear, suggestions that he was on the way on an active nuclear program. David Kay, "We have not discovered significant evidence of—"

Bush: Yet.

Sawyer: Is it "yet"?

Bush: But what David Kay did discover was they had a weapons program. And had that—that—*let me finish for a second.* Now it's more extensive than—than missiles. Had that knowledge been examined by the United Nations or had David Kay's report been placed in front of the United Nations, he, Saddam Hussein, would have been in material breach of 1441, which meant it was a *causis belli* [which should be *causa belli*]. And, look, *there is no doubt* that

Saddam Hussein was a dangerous person. And *there's no doubt* we had a body of evidence proving that. And *there is no doubt* that the President must act, after 9/11, to make America a more secure country.

Sawyer: Again, I'm just trying to ask—these are supporters, people who believed in the war who have asked the question.

Bush: *Well, you can keep asking the question. And my answer's gonna be the same. Saddam was a danger. And the world is better off because we got rid of him.*

Sawyer: But stated as a hard fact, that there were weapons of mass destruction as opposed to the possibility that he could move to acquire those weapons still.

Bush: *So what's the difference?*

Sawyer: Well—

Bush: The possibility that he could acquire weapons. If he were to acquire weapons, he would be the danger. That's, that's what I'm trying to explain to you. A gathering threat, after 9/11, is a threat that needed to be dealt with. And it was done after 12 long years of the world saying the man's a danger. And so, we got rid of him. And there's no doubt the world is a safer, freer place as a result of Saddam being gone.

Sawyer: But—but, again, some—some of the critics have said this, combined with the failure to establish proof of elaborate terrorism contacts, has indicated that there's just not precision, at best, and misleading, at worst.

Bush: Yeah. Look—what—what we based our evidence on was a very sound national intelligence estimate.

Sawyer: Nothing should have been more precise?

Bush: I—I made my decision based upon enough intelligence to tell me that *this country was threatened with Saddam Hussein in power.*

Sawyer: What would it take to convince you he didn't have weapons of mass destruction?

Bush: *Saddam Hussein was a threat. And the fact that he is gone means America is a safer country.*

Sawyer: And if he doesn't have weapons of mass destruction?

Bush: *Diane, you can keep asking the question. I'm telling you, I made the right decision for America. Because Saddam Hussein used weapons of mass destruction, invaded Kuwait. But the fact that he is not there is—means America's a more secure country.*

Dec. 16, 2003

Ad Hominem

An *ad hominem* argument literally is an argument "against the man". Here one attack's a person's character, qualifications, intentions, or motives instead of showing why this person's views on behalf of some claim are incorrect.

In the first debate with Gore, the vice-president's character is assailed as he at least implicitly links Gore to Clinton with a comment about the Lincoln bedroom. To his credit, Gore does not reply with an attack on Bush's character.

Lehrer: New question. Are there issues of character that distinguish you from Vice President Gore?

Bush: The man loves his wife and I appreciate that a lot. And I love mine. The man loves his family a lot, and I appreciate that, because I love my family. I think the thing that discouraged me about the vice president was uttering those famous words, "No controlling legal authority". I felt like there needed to be a better sense of responsibility of what was going on in the White House. *I believe that—I believe they've moved that sign, "The buck stops here" from the Oval Office desk to "The buck stops here" on the Lincoln bedroom.* It's not good for the country and it's not right. We need to have a new look about how we conduct ourselves in office. There's a huge trust. I see it all the time when people come up to me and say, I don't want you to let me down again. And we can do better than the past administration has done. It's time for a fresh start. It's time for a new look. It's time for a fresh start after a season of cynicism. And so *I don't know the man well, but I've been disappointed about how he and his administration have conducted the fundraising affairs. You know, going to a Buddhist temple and then claiming it wasn't a fundraiser isn't my view of responsibility.*

Lehrer: Vice President Gore?

Gore: *I think we ought to attack our country's problems, not attack each other.* I want to spend my time making this country even better than it is, not trying to make you out to be a bad person. You may want to focus on scandal. I want to focus on results. As I said a couple of months ago, I

> stand here as my own man and I want you to see me for who I really am. Tipper and I have been married for 30 years. We became grandparents a year-and-a-half ago. We've got four children. I have devoted 24 years of my life to public service and I've said this before and I'll say it again, if you entrust me with the presidency, I may not be the most exciting politician, but I will work hard for you every day. I will fight for middle-class families and working men and women and I will never let you down.
>
> Oct. 3, 2000

The flip-flopping attack on John Kerry is also an instance of an *ad hominem* attack.

Bush: Only four United States senators voted to authorize the use of force, and then voted against funding our troops—only four—and two of those senators were my opponent and his running mate. When asked to explain his decision, he said, "*I actually did vote for the $87 billion before I voted against it*".

Audience: Booo!

Bush: I suspect here—I suspect here in Poplar Bluff, not many people talk that way. They then pressed him, and he said he's proud of his vote. And finally, he said it was a complicated matter. There's nothing complicated about supporting our troops in combat. *After voting for the war, but against funding it, after saying he would have voted for the war even knowing everything we know today, my opponent woke up this morning with new campaign advisors, and yet another new position. Suddenly, he's against it again.*

Audience: Flip-flop! Flip-Flop! Flip-flop!

Bush: No matter how many times Senator Kerry changes his mind, it was right for America then, and it's right for America now that Saddam Hussein is no longer in power.

Poplar Bluff, MO, Sept. 6, 2004

And again, just weeks later.

> You know, later on this week, I'm going to have a chance to debate my opponent [John Kerry]. It's been a little tough to prepare, because *he keeps changing positions on the war on terror.* He voted for the use of force in Iraq, and then didn't—didn't vote to fund the troops. He com-

> plained that we're not spending enough money to help in the reconstruction of Iraq, and now he's saying we're spending too much. He said it was the right decision to go into Iraq. Now he calls it the wrong war—*probably could spend 90 minutes debating himself.*
>
> Springfield, OH, Sept. 27, 2004

What Bush fails to relate is that Kerry's "nay" vote to fund the troops in Iraq was based on additional evidence he did not have at his disposal when he initially voted for war. To flip-flop is to change one's mind *on inspection of the same evidence*. To change one's mind on account of new evidence is not flip-flopping, but a move that is often required by rational thinking.

In a question concerning the rising cost of health care in his second debate with John Kerry, Bush replied irrelevantly and in *ad hominem* fashion.

> Let me see where to start here. First, the National Journal named *Senator Kennedy the most liberal senator of all.* And that's saying something in that bunch. You might say that took a lot of hard work. The reason I bring that up is because he's [Kerry] proposed $2.2 trillion in new spending, and he says he going to tax the rich to close the tax gap. He can't. He's going to tax everybody here to fund his programs. That's just reality.

After criticizing Kerry's voting record, Bush added rhetorically:

> You know, there's a main stream in American politics and *you sit right on the far left bank. As a matter of fact, your record is such that Ted Kennedy, your colleague, is the conservative senator from Massachusetts.*
>
> Oct. 8, 2004

The "liberal" label is old, tiresome, and meaningless, but still it strikes a chord with a great many voters, since many people vote on emotion, not reason.

In his third debate, there came other *ad hominem* attacks in reference to social security:

> He talks about PAYGO. I'll tell you what PAYGO means, when you're a senator from Massachusetts, *when you're a colleague of Ted Kennedy,* pay go means: You pay, and he goes ahead and spends.

> Two things. One, he clearly has a litmus test for his judges, which I disagree with. And secondly, *only a liberal senator from Massachusetts would say that a 49 percent increase in funding for education was not enough.*
>
> Oct. 13, 2004

Swamping

Swamping is perhaps a non-intentional technique of Bush. When pressed or confused, which unfortunately happens all too frequently, the president "answers" a question by throwing out a litany of thoughts that are irrelevant to the question in an attempt to drown or bedazzle an adversary in irrelevancies.

> Hume: When things go badly, as many people would feel they have been in Iraq with the continuing casualties and struggles and difficulties, do you ever doubt [your faith]?
>
> Bush: I don't think they're going badly. I mean, obviously I think they're going badly for the soldiers who lost their lives, and I weep for that person and their family. But no, I think we're making good progress. As I said I pray for calmness when the seas are storming, and I—you know, my faith is an integral part of being who I am, and I'm not going to change.
>
> Interview with Brit Hume, Sept. 22, 2003

First, Bush immediately goes off the topic of doubting his faith by stating things are not going badly. Secondly, he qualifies this statement by adding that they are going badly for those who have lost their lives, and when the topic of lost lives comes up, thirdly, he finds that he needs to say something about weeping for the dead soldiers. He is, after all, a "*compassionate* conservative", if nothing else. Fourthly, he returns to the issue of things not going badly by adding one of his favorite timeworn statements, "we're making progress". Fifthly, he returns back to praying, which he talked about prior to this question. Sixthly, he states that his faith is a part of him. Finally, he ends with a not unfamiliar statement, "I'm not going to change". In the end Bush never straightforwardly addresses the question. The interviewer may by this time be so tired or confounded that he pushes forward to the next question or just gives up in utter frustration.

Straw Man

To create a straw man is to misrepresenting another's position by weakening it in order to show it to be untenable. I give one instance below.

> I'm absolutely opposed to a national health care plan. I don't want the federal government making decisions for consumers or for providers. I remember what the administration tried to do in 1993. *They [Clinton and Gore] tried to have a national health care plan.* And fortunately, it failed. I trust people, I don't trust the federal government. It's going to be one of the themes you hear tonight. I don't want the federal government making decisions on behalf of everybody.
>
> Bush/Gore III, Oct. 17, 2000

Bush consistently characterized the Clinton health-care plan as a "national health care plan". It was not.

Chapter 7
Rule II: Never Take a Blow Straight-On

"'Have you guessed the riddle yet?' the Hatter said, turning to Alice again.
"'No, I give it up', Alice replied. 'What's the answer?'
"'I haven't the slightest idea', said the Hatter".

A second group of rhetorical devices comprise a number of defensive, deflection strategies. I list six below.

Ignore/Bypass the Question

Consider this instance of bypassing a question by Diane Sawyer.

Sawyer: Mrs. Clinton has said it's time for the American people to write their senators and congressmen and say, "Buck the gun lobby". Do you want Americans to write their senators and say that?

Bush: *I don't know what that means. I do know that* mothers and dads have got to say and understand the most important job

> they will ever have—they will ever have—is to love their children.
>
> *Good Morning America*, May 10, 1999

Below, Bush wholly ignores Brit Hume's question and answers one that is not asked.

> Hume: Do you think that President Bush [senior] could have done the job he did in assembling and holding together the Gulf War coalition, composed of many very varied nations, had he not had the knowledge of the world that he had from years of experience and diplomacy and politics at the UN?
>
> Bush: In order to be a good president when it comes to foreign policy, it requires someone with vision, judgment, and leadership. I've been the governor of the second biggest state in the United States. If it were a nation, it would be the eleventh largest economy in the world. I was overwhelmingly reelected because the people in my state realized I know how to lead, and I've shown good judgment. A couple of weeks ago, at the Reagan Library, I talked about my vision for peace. My goal, should I become the president, is to keep the peace. I intend to do so by promoting free trade, which, in my judgment, promotes American values across the world. I intend to do so by strengthening alliances, which says America cannot go alone; we must be peacemakers, not peace-keepers. And I intend to strengthen the military to make sure that the world is peaceful.
>
> Hume: With all respect, sir, I don't think you answered the question.
>
> Bush: *Well, I gave you my qualifications why I think I'll be a good foreign policy leader.*
>
> GOP Debate, New Hampshire, Dec. 2, 1999

The reply, entirely beside the point, should come as no surprise. Bush has merely shifted discussion to his favorite topic: himself.

In his first debate with John Kerry, Bush again ignores the question asked and begins to talk about himself.

> Question: Do you believe the election of Senator Kerry on November the 2nd would increase the chances of the U.S. being hit by another 9/11-type terrorist attack?

Bush: No, *I don't believe it's going to happen.* I believe I'm going to win, because the American people know I know how to lead. I've shown the American people I know how to lead. I have—I understand everybody in this country doesn't agree with the decisions I've made. And I made some tough decisions. But people know where I stand. People out there listening know what I believe. And that's how best it is to keep the peace. This nation of ours has got a solemn duty to defeat this ideology of hate. And that's what they are. This is a group of killers who will not only kill here, but kill children in Russia, that'll attack unmercifully in Iraq, hoping to shake our will. We have a duty to defeat this enemy. We have a duty to protect our children and grandchildren. The best way to defeat them is to never waver, to be strong, to use every asset at our disposal, *is to constantly stay on the offensive and, at the same time, spread liberty.* And that's what people are seeing now is happening in Afghanistan. Ten million citizens have registered to vote. It's a phenomenal statistic. They're given a chance to be free, and they will show up at the polls. Forty-one percent of those 10 million are women. In Iraq, no doubt about it, *it's tough. It's hard work. It's incredibly hard.* You know why? Because an enemy realizes the stakes. The enemy understands a free Iraq will be a major defeat in their ideology of hatred. That's why they're fighting so vociferously. *They showed up* in Afghanistan when they were there, because they tried to beat us and they didn't. And *they're showing up* in Iraq for the same reason. They're trying to defeat us. And if we lose our will, we lose. But if we remain strong and resolute, we will defeat this enemy.

Sept. 30, 2004

In his first debate with Al Gore, Bush deflected a question on Supreme Court nominees and the pro-life issue.

Lehrer: Should a voter assume that all judicial appointments you make to the Supreme Court or any other court, federal court, will also be pro-life?

Bush: The voters should assume I have no litmus test on that issue or any other issue. Voters will know I'll put competent judges on the bench. People who will strictly interpret the Constitution and not use the bench for writing social

> policy. That is going to be a big difference between my opponent and me. I believe that the judges ought not to take the place of the legislative branch of government. That they're appointed for life and that they ought to look at the Constitution as sacred. They shouldn't misuse their bench. I don't believe in liberal activist judges. I believe in strict constructionists. Those are the kind of judges I will appoint. I've named four in the State of Texas and ask the people to check out their qualifications, their deliberations. They're good, solid men and women who have made good, sound judgments on behalf of the people of Texas.
>
> Oct. 3, 2000

In a press conference two months later, Bush is caught off-guard by a question about which he knows nothing. His reply is clumsy, evasive, and dishonest.

Reporter:	The European Union and Japan have filed a challenge to the WTO against a rule in the Agriculture Appropriations Bill that would allow steel companies to receive money from antidumping duties.
Bush:	*Say again now?*
Reporter:	It's an agriculture appropriations bill. President Clinton opposes this language in there that would allow companies to receive receipts from antidumping duties.
Bush:	*I think the administration needs to do what they think is right, and I'll address all these issues once I'm sworn in as the president.*

Dec. 22, 2000

His final comment might be more succinctly expressed as "Say what?"

In a press conference in Paris, France, in 2002, Bush ignores a particularly thorny question by a reporter.

Question:	Mr. President, Mr. Bush, after your trip to Russia, what would be for you a more decisive ally in your war against terrorism? Would it be Russia, or this little corner of this continent which is called Western Europe? And please, Mr. President, don't say "both"—this wouldn't be the beginning of an answer.

Bush:	Both. (Yucks.) What was that? I didn't get the full question. I got "Russia", and I got "this little corner of Europe". But what was the question, "Who [*sic*] do I rely on more?"
Reporter:	What is for you the more decisive ally in your war against terrorism?
Bush:	Decisive ally? Ally? Decisive ally? Of course, Jacques Chirac. Yucks. I—listen, thank you for the trick question. *Let me talk about this ally.* The phone rang the day after the attack—the day of the attack. I can't remember exactly when, but it was immediately [*sic*]. And he said, "I'm your friend". On this continent, France takes the lead in helping to hunt down people who want to harm America and/or the French, or anybody else.

Paris, May 26, 2002

Finally, in a press conference in 2003, Bush tries to use humor to duck a question on the number of troops in Iraq—one that he has consistently evaded, as we've seen in chapter one, with lines such as "they'll come back when the job is done".

Reporter:	You recently put Condoleezza Rice, your National Security Advisor, in charge of the management of the administration's Iraq policy. What has effectively changed since she's been in charge? And the second question, can you promise a year from now that you will have reduced the number of troops in Iraq?
Bush:	The second question is a trick question, so I won't answer it.... (Yucks.)

Oct. 28, 2003

Change the Topic (Red Herring)

Another favorite deflection strategy of Bush is changing the topic to one more suited to him. Consider the following exchange between Juan Williams and the president over Bush's refusal to take a personal stand on whether the people of South Carolina should fly the confederate flag, in spite of the fact that it's a symbol of racism to many Americans. Bush clumsily changes the topic in rote fashion to a handful of unrelated issues.

Williams:	[Y]our stand on the flag issue in South Carolina. You said, "It's up to the people of South Carolina"—as if you have no historical context, as if you don't have a position there of your own.
Bush:	Juan, I've got a position.
Williams:	Your position is: Leave it up to the people.
Bush:	*No, no, my position is the people of South Carolina can decide.* [huh?] You may not like my position, but that's a position. *And I don't believe the polls said that. I don't read the polls. But I suspect that when you look closely at what the people of this state like, they like somebody who tells them exactly what my record is, what my philosophy is. I don't make decisions based upon polls or focus groups, Juan. I'm the person who laid out a tax-cut plan that has stood the test of time. I'm not the candidate that, when the heat got on, started, kind of, fine-tuning the tax-cut plan.*

Fox News Sunday, January 30, 2000

When asked for his position of gun laws during the second Bush/Gore Debate of 2000, the governor, so to speak, beat around the bush for a while before changing the topic entirely to something not so unfriendly to him. Note the final and decisive rhetorical move, "Guns laws are important, *but so is x*", where *x* can stand for any topic to which he wants the conversation to turn.

> Well, I'm not for photo licensing. Let me say something about Columbine. Listen, we've got gun laws. He says we ought to have gun-free schools. Everybody believes that. I'm sure every state in the union has got them. You can't carry a gun into a school. And there ought to be a consequence when you do carry a gun into a school. But Columbine spoke to a larger issue. It's really a matter of culture. It's a culture that somewhere along the line *we've begun to disrespect life*. Where a child can walk in and have their heart turned dark as a result of being on the Internet and walk in and decide to take somebody else's life? So gun laws are important, no question about it, *but so is [*sic*] loving children, and character education classes, and faith-based programs being a part of after-school programs.* Some desperate child needs to have somebody

put their arm around them and say, we love you. So there's a—this is a society that—of ours that's got to do a better job of teaching children right from wrong. And we can enforce law. But there seems to be a lot of preoccupation on—not certainly only in this debate, but just in general on law. But there's a larger law. Love your neighbor like you would like to be loved yourself. And that's where our society must head if we're going to be a peaceful and prosperous society.

Oct. 11, 2000

In a press conference with Polish president Kwasniewski, Bush was hit head on by a question concerning the possibility of shady business practices on behalf of himself and Cheney.

Reporter: Mr. President, even while you're calling for transparency in corporate America, you refuse to ask the SEC to turn over documents from its investigation into Harken Energy Corporation, your old company. And the Vice President has answered few questions about his role at Halliburton, his old company, which is now under investigation by the SEC. Why not just clear the air, ask the SEC to release those documents, and ask the Vice President to talk about Halliburton in a public forum?

Bush: Well, first—the Vice President—I've got great confidence in the Vice President—doing a heck of a good job. When I picked him, I knew he was a fine business leader and a fine experienced man. And he's doing a great job. That matter will take—run its course—the Halliburton investigation—and the facts will come out at some point in time.

Secondly, as to a look at Harken, the SEC, as a result of Freedom of Information requests, has released documents, and the key document said there is no case. It was fully investigated by career investigators. Some of you, I think, have talked to the head career investigator, and he's made it clear there was no case.

The key thing for the American people is to realize that the fundamentals for economic vitality and growth are there: low interest rates, good monetary policy, productivity increases, economic vitality and growth in the first quarter. And that, as Chairman Greenspan said yesterday, that we've got to change from a culture of greed to a culture of responsibility. And I believe that's going to happen.

July 17, 2002

In the first paragraph, Bush in effect stalls for time and says nothing about Cheney's involvement with Halliburton. In the second paragraph, he skirts the issue through misleading. It is now common knowledge that the president was involved in suspicious business dealings with Harken. Hired as a consultant for Harken in 1986, he received about $500,000 in their stock and earned $120,000 as a salary. He sold 212,000 Harken shares of stock in 1990 for $4.00 per share and pocketed a total of $848,000 just prior to the word getting out publicly that Harken would lose roughly 4,200,000 in 1989. Coincidence? Bush used the profit to pay off a $500,000 bank loan he'd taken out the year before to buy a part of the Texas Rangers baseball team. The SEC "investigated", but did not find that Bush possessed insider information. In the final paragraph, he turns completely away from the issue and talks about economic growth and fiscal responsibility.

One of the best examples of a red herring comes in the third debate with Kerry on the issue of the minimum wage. The question was about the ever-growing gap between rich and poor in America. Unsurprisingly, Bush completely dodged the question and went on to talk about reform of education.

> Actually, Mitch McConnell had a minimum-wage plan that I supported that would have increased the minimum wage. *But let me talk about what's really important for the worker you're referring to. And that's to make sure the education system works.* It's to make sure we raise standards. Listen, the No Child Left Behind Act is really a jobs act when you think about it. The No Child Left Behind Act says, "We'll raise standards. We'll increase federal spending". But in return for extra spending, we now want people to measure—states and local jurisdictions to measure to show us whether or not a child can read or write or add and subtract. You cannot solve a problem unless you diagnose the problem. And we weren't diagnosing problems. And therefore just kids were being shuffled through the school. And guess who would get shuffled through? Children whose parents wouldn't speak English as a first language just move through. Many inner-city kids just move through. We've stopped that practice now by measuring early. And when we find a problem, we spend extra money to correct it. I remember a lady in Houston, Texas,

> told me, "Reading is the new civil right", and she's right. In order to make sure people have jobs for the 21st century, we've got to get it right in the education system, and we're beginning to close a minority achievement gap now. You see, we'll never be able to compete in the 21st century unless we have an education system that doesn't quit on children, an education system that raises standards, an education that makes sure there's excellence in every classroom.
>
> Oct. 17, 2004

Finally, There is an interview with Tim Russert on *Meet the Press.*

Russert:	Will you testify before the [9/11] commission?
Bush:	This commission? You know, testify? I mean, I'd be glad to visit with them. I'd be glad to share with them knowledge. I'd be glad to make recommendations, if they ask for some. I'm interested in getting—I'm interested in making sure the intelligence gathering works well. Listen, we got some fine—let me—let me, again, just give you a sense of where I am on the intelligence systems of America. First of all, I strongly believe the CIA is ably led by George Tenet. He comes and briefs me on a regular basis about what he and his analysts see in the world.

Feb. 7, 2004

Slanting

To slant is to deliberately omit, deemphasize, or overemphasize some point in an effort to conceal the truth of the matter. A good example of this occurred in Bush/Kerry II. Bush—when asked about the type of Supreme-Court judge he would appoint, if he should be in a position to appoint one—gave examples of the type of person he *wouldn't* pick. The real issue here was whether he'd appoint someone who was radically conservative. The false humor and dissimulation are atrocious.

> I'm not telling. I really don't have—haven't picked anybody yet. [Yuck, yuck!] Plus, I want them all voting for me. [More yucks!] I would pick

> somebody who would not allow their personal opinion to get in the way of the law. I would pick somebody who would strictly interpret the Constitution of the United States. *Let me give you a couple of examples, I guess, of the kind of person I wouldn't pick.* I wouldn't pick a judge who said that the Pledge of Allegiance couldn't be said in a school because it had the words "under God" in it. I think that's an example of a judge allowing personal opinion to enter into the decision-making process as opposed to a strict interpretation of the Constitution. Another example would be the Dred Scott case, which is where judges, years ago, said that the Constitution allowed slavery because of personal property rights. That's a personal opinion. That's not what the Constitution says. The Constitution of the United States says we're all—you know, it doesn't say that. It doesn't speak to the equality of America. And so, I would pick people that would be strict constructionists. We've got plenty of lawmakers in Washington, D.C. Legislators make law; judges interpret the Constitution. And I suspect one of us will have a pick at the end of next year—the next four years. And that's the kind of judge I'm going to put on there. No litmus test except for how they interpret the Constitution.

Kerry struck back cleverly saying:

> A few years ago when he came to office, the president said—these are his words—"What we need are some good conservative judges on the courts". And he said also that his two favorite justices are Justice Scalia and Justice Thomas. So you get a pretty good sense of where he's heading, if he were to appoint somebody.
>
> Oct. 8, 2004

On *Meet the Press*, Bush tries to justify the invasion of Iraq by appealing to some possible, dangerous state of affairs in the indefinite future.

> I repeat to you what I strongly believe that *inaction in Iraq would have emboldened Saddam Hussein.* He could have developed a nuclear weapon over time—I'm not saying immediately, but over time—which would then have put us in what position? *We would have been in a position of blackmail.* In other words, you can't rely upon a madman, and he was a madman. You can't rely upon him making rational decisions when it comes to war and peace, and it's too late, in my judgment, when a madman who has got terrorist connections is able to act.
>
> Feb. 7, 2004

This is, of course, the very same situation we are now in with North Korea, due to U.S. inaction. Moreover, this "madman", Hussein, was given helicopters and biological weapons by the Reagan administration in a war with Iran in the 1980s. Why *then* was he so trustworthy and why *now* has he become so untrustworthy?

In a press conference in April of 2004, Bush was asked about his refusal to admit that he ever errs.

> Reporter: One of the biggest criticisms of you is that whether it's WMD in Iraq, postwar planning in Iraq, or even the question of whether this administration did enough to ward off 9/11, *you never admit a mistake. Is that a fair criticism, and do you believe that there were any errors in judgment that you made related to any of those topics I brought up?*
>
> Bush: Well, I think, as I mentioned, you know, the country wasn't on war footing, and yet we're at war. And that's just a reality, Dave. I mean, that was the situation that existed prior to 9/11, because the truth of the matter is most in the country never felt that we'd be vulnerable to an attack such as the one that Osama bin Laden unleashed on us. We knew he had designs on us. We knew he hated us. But there was nobody in our government, at least, and I don't think the prior government that could envision flying airplanes into buildings on such a massive scale. The people know where I stand, I mean, in terms of Iraq. I was very clear about what I believed. And, of course, I want to know why we haven't found a weapon yet. But I still know Saddam Hussein was a threat. And the world is better off without Saddam Hussein. I don't think anybody can—maybe people can argue that. I know the Iraqi people don't believe that, that they're better off with Saddam Hussein—would be better off with Saddam Hussein in power.
>
> Apr. 13, 2004

Finally, when asked why he did not treat Yasser Arafat, whom Bush considers to be a terrorist, as he's treated other terrorists, like Hussein, Bush replied:

> Well, not every action requires military action, Jim. As you noticed, for

> example in North Korea, we've chosen to put together a multinational strategy to deal with Mr. Kim Jong-Il. Not every action requires military action. As a matter of fact, military action is the very last resort for us. And a reminder: When you mentioned Saddam Hussein, I just wanted to remind you that the Saddam Hussein military action took place after innumerable United Nations Security Council resolutions were passed—not one, two or three, but a lot. And so, this nation is very reluctant to use military force. We try to enforce doctrine peacefully, or through alliances or multinational forums. And we will continue to do so.
>
> The Rose Garden, Oct. 28, 2003

The long and the short of it? The U.S. military is already spread too thin.

"It's Hard Work"

And then, of course, if none of the above defective strategies works, one can always appeal to the difficulty of the task at hand. The it's-hard-work line, for instance, paid dividends as a rhetorical device in the first Bush/Kerry debate, on September 30 of 2004, to describe what's being done and what has to be done since the attack and Iraqification of Iraq. Here are several examples.

> In Iraq, no doubt about it—*it's tough. It's hard work. It's incredibly hard.* You know why? Because an enemy realizes the stakes. The enemy understands a free Iraq will be a major defeat in their ideology of hatred. That's why they're fighting so vociferously.

> Of course we're doing everything we can to protect America. I wake up every day thinking about how best to protect America. That's my job. I work with Director Mueller of the FBI; comes in my office when I'm in Washington every morning, talking about how to protect us. *There's* a lot of really good people [sic] *working hard* to do so. *It's hard work.*

> No, what I said was that, because we achieved such a rapid victory, more of the Saddam loyalists were around. I mean, we thought we'd whip more of them going in. But because Tommy Franks did such a great job

> in planning the operation, we moved rapidly, and a lot of the Baathists and Saddam loyalists laid down their arms and disappeared. I thought they would stay and fight, but they didn't. And now we're fighting them now. And *it's hard work.* I understand *how hard it is.* I get the casualty reports every day. I see on the TV screens *how hard it is.*
>
> We've got a plan in place. *The plan says* there will be elections in January, and there will be. *The plan says* we'll train Iraqi soldiers so they can *do the hard work*, and we are. And it's not only just America, but NATO is now helping, Jordan's helping train police, UAE is helping train police. We've allocated $7 billion over the next months for reconstruction efforts. And *we're making progress* there. And our alliance is strong. And as I just told you, there's going to be a summit of the Arab nations. Japan will be hosting a summit. We're making progress. *It is hard work. It is hard work* to go from a tyranny to a democracy. *It's hard work* to go from a place where people get their hands cut off, or executed, to a place where people are free. But *it's necessary work.* And a free Iraq is going to make this world a more peaceful place.
>
> You know, I think about Missy Johnson. She's a fantastic lady I met in Charlotte, North Carolina. She and her son Bryan, they came to see me. Her husband PJ got killed. He'd been in Afghanistan, went to Iraq. You know, *it's hard work* to try to love her as best as I can, knowing full well that the decision I made caused her loved one to be in harm's way.
>
> Yes, we're getting the job done [in Iraq]. *It's hard work.* Everybody knows *it's hard work*, because there's a determined enemy that's trying to defeat us.
>
> We've done *a lot of hard work* together over the last three and a half years. We've been challenged, and we've risen to those challenges. We've climbed the mighty mountain. I see the valley below, and it's a valley of peace. By being steadfast and resolute and strong, by keeping our word, by supporting our troops, we can achieve the peace we all want.

Cover Your Ass

Finally, no matter what happens, Bush is always sure that no one will be able to link him with any wrongdoing. Consider once again what Bush said about sharing his administration's policies with Congress and the public in general in a 2002 press conference. I cannot help but have a little fun here by adding my own take on what Bush would have actually said in brackets, if he had had an inflexible commitment to truth.

> Reporter: Given that you've not convinced everyone in your own party of that [that Bush's administration freely shares information on its energy policy with Congress], to what degree are you trying to recalibrate the power between Congress and the presidency?
>
> Bush: First of all, I'm not going to let Congress erode the power of the executive branch [*i.e., I want power!*] I have a duty to protect the executive branch from legislative encroachment [*i.e., I crave power!*]. I mean, for example, when the GAO demands documents from us, we're not going to give them to them [*i.e., I've got plenty to hide*]. I mean, it's just—you know—these were privileged conversations [*i.e., no chance of getting reelected, if these leak out*]. These were conversations when people come into our offices and brief us. And can you imagine having to give up every single transcript of what has advised me or the vice president? [*i.e., shit would hit the fan*] Our advice wouldn't be good and honest and open [*i.e., the public would see what a bunch of imperialistic schemers we really are*]. And so I viewed that as an encroachment on the power of the executive branch. I have an obligation to make sure that the presidency remains robust and that the legislative branch doesn't end up running the executive branch [i.e., in Bush's own words: "*If this were a dictatorship, it'd be a heck of a lot easier, just so long as I'm the dictator*"].
>
> Mar. 13, 2002

Finally, at another press conference the following year, Bush is confronted with turning over White-House documents relating to what the administration knew about a potential terrorist attack, prior to 9/11. Bush replies in superb cover-my-ass fashion. Again I add my own take on things in brackets.

Reporter: Mr. President, thank you. As you know, the Chairman of the commission investigating the September 11 attacks wants documents from the White House, and said this week that he might have to use subpoena power. You have said there's some national security concerns about turning over some of those documents to people outside of the Executive Branch. Will you turn them over, or can you at least outline for the American people what you think is a reasonable compromise so that the commission learns what it needs to know, and you protect national security, if you think it's that important?

Bush: Yes. It is important for me to protect national security [*i.e., to cover my own ass!*]. You're talking about the presidential daily brief. It's important for the writers of the presidential daily brief to feel comfortable that the documents will never be politicized and/or unnecessarily exposed for public purview [*i.e., we've got plenty to hide*]. I—and so, therefore, the kind of the first statements out of this administration were very protective of the presidential prerogatives of the past and to protect the right for other presidents, future presidents, to have a good presidential daily brief [*i.e., I don't care what happens once* I *leave office*].

Oct. 28, 2003

Chapter 8
Rule III: Confuse or Tire Out Your Adversary

> *"'I quite agree with you', said the Duchess; 'and the moral of that is—"Be what you would seem to be"—or, if you'd like it put more simply—"Never imagine yourself not to be otherwise than what it might appear to others that what you were or might have been was not otherwise than what you had been would have appeared to them to be otherwise"'".*

Marcus Cicero wrote some 2,000 years ago:

> For as a flowing stream is corrupted either with difficulty or not at all, however confined water is easily corrupted; thus with a river of eloquence the censures of refutation are removed, however the poverty of confined reason does not defend itself easily.[1]

For the ancient orators around the time of Cicero, obscurity was a sign of eloquence and it had the secondary advantage of making one's position difficult to attack.

---

1 My translation. Cicero, *Tusculan Orations* II.lv.7.

In tacit agreement with Cicero, though from insalubrious motives, a third rule Bush unabashedly adopts is to create an atmosphere of tedium through confusion or tiresome rhetorical devices, whenever possible. He uses a number of methods to do this. I list five below.

Repetition

In the first debate with Al Gore, note the rhetorical force of "surely" before the first four sentences.

> *Surely* this nation can come together to promote the value of life. *Surely* we can fight off these laws that will encourage doctors to—to allow doctors to take the lives of our seniors. *Surely* we can work together to create a cultural life so some of these youngsters who feel like they can take a neighbor's life with a gun will understand that that's not the way America is meant to be. *Surely* we can find common ground to reduce the number of abortions in America. As to the drug itself, I mentioned I was disappointed. I hope the FDA took its time to make sure that American women will be safe who use this drug.
>
> Oct. 3, 2000

Consider Bush's use of certain key phrases that were repeated *ad nauseum* in his first debate with Kerry.

> You can't expect to build an alliance *when you denigrate the contributions* of those who are serving side by side with American troops in Iraq. Plus, he says the cornerstone of his plan to succeed in Iraq is to call upon nations to serve. So what's the message going to be: "Please join us in Iraq. We're a grand diversion. Join us for a war that is *the wrong war at the wrong place at the wrong time?*" I know how these people think. I deal with them all the time. I sit down with the world leaders frequently and talk to them on the phone frequently. *They're not going to follow somebody* who says, "*This is the wrong war at the wrong place at the wrong time*". *They're not going to follow somebody whose core convictions keep changing* because of politics in America.
>
> Sept. 30, 2004

The phrase, "wrong war…wrong place…wrong time" (see chapter 5), for instance, was repeated six times in the first debate, but thereafter used sparingly. The "fuzzy math" theme, which we'll come to next, was repeated four times in this same debate and was hinted at very early on as Bush declared prefatorily, "Let me just say that obviously tonight we're going to hear some phony numbers about what I think and what we ought to do". The phrase "scare/frighten people into the voting booth" was used four times.

Also in debate one, notice how the *ad hominem* attack on Kerry occurs through the use of repetition.

> My opponent calls it a mistake. It wasn't a mistake. He said *I misled* on Iraq. *I don't think he was misleading* when he called Iraq a grave threat in the fall of 2002. *I don't think he was misleading* when he said that it was right to disarm Iraq in the spring of 2003. *I don't think he misled* you when he said that, you know, anyone who doubted whether the world was better off without Saddam Hussein in power didn't have the judgment to be president. *I don't think he was misleading. I think what is misleading* is to say you can lead and succeed in Iraq if you keep changing your positions on this war.

When asked in the same debate, when the troops would come home, Bush merely replied:

> *A free Iraq* will be an ally in the war on terror, and that's essential. *A free Iraq* will set a powerful example in the part of the world that is desperate for freedom. *A free Iraq* will help secure Israel. *A free Iraq* will enforce the hopes and aspirations of the reformers in places like Iran. *A free Iraq* is essential for the security of this country.

In the following passage, Bush's use of "certain" and "uncertain", whether intentional or accidental, is dizzying, to say the least.

> This is a world that is much more *uncertain* than the past. In the past we were *certain*, we were *certain* it was us versus the Russians in the past. We were *certain*, and therefore we had huge nuclear arsenals aimed at

> each other to keep the peace. That's what we were *certain* of.... You see, even though it's an *uncertain* world, we're *certain* of some things. We're *certain* that even though the 'evil empire' may have passed, evil still remains. We're *certain* there are people that can't stand what America stands for.... We're *certain* there are madmen in this world, and there's terror, and there's missiles, and I'm *certain* of this, too: I'm *certain* to maintain the peace, we better have a military of high morale, and I'm *certain* that under this administration, morale in the military is dangerously low.
>
> *Washington Post*, May 31, 2000

The appeal to fear, through repeating "dangerous place", is evident in this response to a reporter's question at press conference.

> Reporter: Mr. President, thank you. In recent weeks, you and your White House team have made a concerted effort to put a positive spin on progress in Iraq. At the same time, there's been a much more somber assessment in private, as with Secretary Rumsfeld's memo. And there are people out there who don't believe that the administration is leveling with them about the difficulty and scope of the problem in Iraq.
>
> Bush: Yes, I can't put it any more plainly, *Iraq is a dangerous place.* That's leveling. *It is a dangerous place*.... And *Iraq is dangerous*, and *it's dangerous* because terrorists want us to leave. And we're not leaving.
>
> Oct. 28, 2003

At an informal gathering at Greece Athena Middle and High School in Greece, New York, Bush makes light of his own tendency to repeat.

> As you—as I mentioned to you earlier, we're going to redesign the current system. If you've retired, you don't have anything to worry about—third time I've said that. Yucks. I'll probably say it three more times. See, in my line of work you got to keep repeating things over and over and over again for the truth to sink in—to kind of catapult the propaganda.
>
> May 24, 2005

Finally, when asked in a Cabinet meeting whether Karl Rove acted irresponsibly in talking about Valerie Plame with reporters (chapter 4), potentially a serious crime, Bush used repetition to dodge the issue.

> Mark, I have instructed every member of my staff to fully cooperate [*sic*] in this investigation. I also will not prejudge the investigation based on media reports. We're in the midst of an ongoing investigation, and I will be more than happy to comment further once the investigation is completed.

When the next reporter pressed Bush on the same sensitive issue, the president replied thus, almost robotically:

> We're in the midst of an ongoing investigation, and this is a serious investigation. And it is very important for people not to prejudge the investigation based on media reports. And again, I will be more than happy to comment on this matter once the investigation is complete.
>
> July 13, 2005

"Fuzzy Math"

In the first debate between Bush and Gore, Bush sidestepped any arguments that Gore put forth concerning data in almost mantra-like fashion with the term "fuzzy math" and, in one instance, "Washington fuzzy math". It was a way for Bush to denigrate the position of Gore without addressing the numerical data his opponent was putting forth. It was also a pitiful way of dismissing factual data, relevant to voter's assessment of Bush's capacity to do the job. In the minds of voters and (sorrowfully!) analysts, the tactic worked.

> Look, this is a man who has great numbers. He talks about numbers. I'm beginning to think not only did he invent the Internet, but he invented the calculator. It's *fuzzy math.* It's a scaring—he's trying to scare people in the voting booth.

> The man is practicing *fuzzy math* again. There's differences [*sic*]. Under Vice President Gore's plan, he is going to grow the federal government

> in the largest increase since Lyndon Baines Johnson in 1965. We're talking about a massive government, folks. We're talking about adding to or increasing 200 programs, 20,000 new bureaucrats. Imagine how many IRS agents it is going to take to be able to figure out his targeted tax cut for the middle class that excludes 50 million Americans. There is a huge difference in this campaign. He says he's going to give you tax cuts. 50 million of you won't receive it.
>
> I want to say something. This man has been disparaging my plan with all this [*sic*] *Washington fuzzy math.*
>
> I can't let the man continue with *fuzzy math.* It is 1.3 trillion. It will go to everybody who pays taxes. I'm not going to be the kind of president that says you get tax relief and you don't. I'm not going to be a picker and chooser. What is fair is everybody who pays taxes ought to get relief.
>
> Oct. 3, 2000

Not to be outdone by the first debate, Bush/Gore II also had its share of arithmetical gems. It is noteworthy in this first quote how easily Bush dismisses numerical data as irrelevant, but then appeals to them to show Texas' superiority when it comes to health care.

> *You can quote all the numbers you want,* but I'm telling you we care about our people in Texas. We spent a lot of money to make sure people get health care in the State of Texas, and we're doing a better job than they are at the national level for reducing uninsured.

In the same debate, again note how Bush does not address Gore's data on health insurance for children and tries to turn Gore's numbers into a personal attack.

> Gore: I believe there are 1.4 million children in Texas who do not have health insurance. 600,000 of whom, and maybe some of those have since gotten it, but as of a year ago 600,000 of them were actually eligible for it but they couldn't sign up for it because of the barriers that they had set up. [Lehrer now asks Bush to respond.]
>
> Bush: If he's trying to allege that I'm a hard-hearted person and I don't care about children, he's absolutely wrong. We've spent $4.7 billion a year in the State of Texas for uninsured

> people. And they get health care. Now, it's not the most efficient way to get people health care. But I want to remind you, the number of uninsured in America during their watch has increased. He can make any excuse he wants, but the facts are that we're reducing the number of uninsured percentage of our population. And as the percentage of the population is increasing nationally, somehow the allegation that we don't care and we're going to give money for this interest or that interest and not for children in the State of Texas is totally absurd. Let me just tell you who the jury is. The people of Texas. There's only been one governor ever elected to back-to-back four-year terms, and that was me. And I was able to do so with a lot of Democrat votes, nearly 50% of the Hispanic vote, about 27% of the African-American vote, because people know I'm a conservative person and a compassionate person. So he can throw all the kinds of numbers around. I'm just telling you our state comes together to do what is right. We come together both Republicans and Democrats.
>
> Oct. 11, 2000

In the third debate, in reply to Gore's claim that Bush's proposed $1.6 trillion tax cut would give more money to the wealthiest one percent than "all the new money he budgets for education, health care and national defense combined", Bush had this to say.

> Let me talk about tax relief. If you pay taxes, you ought to get tax relief. The vice-president believes only the right people ought to get tax relief. I don't think that's the role of the president to pick you're right and you're not right. I think if you're going to have tax relief, everybody ought to get it. *And therefore, wealthy people are going to get it.*
>
> Oct. 17, 2001

The inordinate amount of money slated to go the wealthiest Americans was justified by some whacky sort of egalitarian concern that all people, poor and rich, ought to get money. The issue of disproportionate distribution of money to the wealthy that Gore brought up was completely ignored.

In the third debate with Kerry, Bush explained why people

from Mexico cross the border into the U.S. to work. The conditional of the second sentence does not seem to have a consequent (a then-part). The reasoning is incomprehensible.

> Many people are coming to this country for economic reasons. They're coming here to work. If you can make 50 cents in the heart of Mexico, for example, or make $5 here in America, $5—15, you're going to come here if you're worth your salt, if you want to put food on the table for your families. And that's what's happening.
>
> Oct. 13, 2004

Below I list additional passages of interest that relate to numbers:

> Well, *I think you can kind—find all kinds of statistics to make all kinds of cases.* I rest my case on the fact that people in Texas like the job I have done.
>
> CNN, Mar. 8, 2000

> And so one of the areas where I think the average Russian will realize that the stereotypes of America have changed is that it's a spirit of cooperation, not one-upsmanship—that we now understand *one plus one can equal three, as opposed to us and Russia we hope to be zero.*
>
> Nov. 15, 2001

> We've tripled the amount of money—I believe it's from $50 million up to $195 million available.
>
> Lima, Peru, Mar. 23, 2002

> Bush: I am looking forward to working with both Republicans and Democrats to advance a plan that will permanently solve Social Security. There is—I met yesterday with members of the United States Senate, I'm meeting today with members of the House of Representatives to discuss the need to work together to get a—a solution that will fix the problem. And here's the problem: the—as dictated by just math, there is—the system will be in the red in 13 years, and in 2042 the system will be broke. That's because people are living longer, and the number of people paying into the Social Security trust is dwindling. And so, therefore, if you have a child—how old is your child, Carl?
>
> Reporter: Fourteen years old.

Bush:	Yes, 14. Well, if she were—
Reporter:	He, sir.
Bush:	He, excuse me. (Yucks.) I should have done the background check. (Yucks.) She will—when she [*sic*] gets ready to—when she's 50, the system will be broke, if my math is correct [close, but not quite]. In other words, if you have a child who is 25 years old, when that person gets—gets near retirement, the system will be bankrupt. And therefore, it seems like to me—and if we wait, the longer we wait, the more expensive the solution. So, therefore, now is the time to act.

Jan. 26, 2005

Misleading Vividness

This rhetorical tool appeals to shoddy induction. This fallacy occurs when a small amount of exceptionally vivid evidence is used to support a generalization.

> As a result of securing ourselves and ridding the Taliban out of Afghanistan, the Afghan people had elections this weekend. And the first voter was a 19-year-old woman. Think about that. *Freedom is on the march!*
>
> Bush/Kerry III, Oct. 13, 2004

One cannot also help but think about the extraordinary numbers of innocent 19-year-old women who were "accidentally" killed in the bombing of Afghanistan. "Freedom is on the march!"

Rationalizing

Consider the following instance of rationalizing in a rather clever exchange from a 2003 press conference.

Reporter:	Thank you, Mr. President. After more than a year of being accused by your critics of waging war for oil, is it frustrating to now hear some of those same critics demand that

you, essentially, take that oil in the form of loans instead of grants for reconstruction?

Bush: Well, that's exactly the point I made to the members of Congress who have come here to the White House to talk about loans or grants. I said, *let's don't burden Iraq with loans. The only thing they'll be able to repay their loans with is oil.* And, hopefully, we'll get a good solution out of the Congress on this issue. We're making progress. We're working hard with the members to make the case that *it's very important for us not to saddle Iraq with a bunch of debt early in its—in the emergence of a market-oriented economy*, an economy that has been wrecked by Mr. Saddam Hussein. I mean, he just destroyed their economy and destroyed their infrastructure, destroyed their education system, destroyed their medical system, all to keep himself in power. He was the ultimate—

Oct. 28, 2003

The reporter, sucking up, does not challenge the president's reasons for going into Iraq. Oil, of course, played no role whatsoever! Yet Iraq does need to pay the U.S. for its efforts at reconstructing *everything that Saddam Hussein has destroyed.* That's only fair. And, since they have no money, Iraq can just pay the U.S. back with oil. This might work, but it's just a thought. No premeditation. Congress can decide the issue. Egad!

Appeals to Authority

The appeal to authority can be an inductively strong argument—so long as the appeal made meets certain conditions. First, the authority must be an authority in the topic under consideration. A psychotherapist, for instance, who pronounces on epidemiology is out of his terrain and should not be trusted. Second, there must be consensus among experts in that area. Finally, the authority appealed to must be part of that consensus. When any of these conditions are not met, the result is a bad or fallacious appeal to authority.

The usual defense of this sort—a defense that is not at all bad if the authority is of the right sort—is to appeal to another person whose authority on such issues is unquestioned.

> Look, history—shall I give you my talk on history and presidencies? Okay, thank you. I don't—what's interesting is George Washington is now getting a second, or third, or fifth, or tenth look in history. I read the Ellis book, which is a really interesting book [fascinating commentary here!], and—*His Excellency* it's called. And McCullough is writing a book on George Washington, as well. People are constantly evaluating somebody's standing in history, a President's standing in history, based upon events that took place during the presidency, based upon things that happened after the presidency [isn't this what historians do?], based upon—like in my case, hopefully, the march of freedom continues way after my presidency. And so I just don't worry about vindication or standing.
>
> Mar. 16, 2005

This is clearly just another sorry attempt to convince the press and the general public that he, who has plainly articulated his disdain for reading in the past, has been a history buff all along. Again, it's highly unconvincing.

Argumentum Pro Homine

As a sort-of counterpart to the *argumentum ad homimen*, I offer the *argumentum pro homine* (argument on behalf of the man)—a bastard type of appeal to authority, where the authority to which Bush appeals is none other than he himself. Consider what Bush said just prior to his election in 2000 about the possibility of Pat Buchanan leaving the Republican Party.

> I don't want Pat Buchanan to leave the Party. I think it's important, should I be the nominee, to unite the Republican Party. *I'm going to need every vote I can get among Republicans to win the election.*
>
> *New York Times*, Sept. 25, 1999

In response to a prior comment that only those who accept Jesus Christ as their lord and savior can go to heaven, Bush had this to say to Tim Russert:

> Governors don't get to decide who gets to go to heaven. No, sir. God decides who goes to heaven, Mr. Russert—God decides. And far be it from *the* politician who tries to play God.
>
> GOP Debate, Durham, Jan. 6, 2000

Perhaps this is a not-so-innocuous slip that is suggestive of an egomaniacal personality? Maybe not, but it's a thought.

In the following exchange, Bush deflects criticism of the consumer confidence index by an appeal to his "own consumer confidence index".

> Reporter: Mr. President, are you concerned at all that consumer confidence, which came in at kind of a low number yesterday, is a harbinger of things to come, particularly as people watch their stock portfolios erode and vanish? Will this make them less likely to spend, and put more pressure on the recovery?
>
> Bush: I think—look, *let me just give you my own consumer confidence index. I am positive about the—our economy. I feel very optimistic about it, because I look at the facts.* And the facts are that inflation is low, interest rates low, productivity is high. We're going to get a trade bill which will help, presuming the Senate acts this week. I feel strongly that they're—that having—now it turns out, having been through three-quarters of negative growth, when I first came into office we've had three-quarters of positive growth, I think that's the right trend, Dick. So I'm optimistic about this, and I think when the American people take a look at the facts and are confident about those facts, like I am, they will—they're going to realize we've got a bright future ahead of us.
>
> July 31, 2002

Argumentum Pro Deo

One of Bush's most canny rhetorical devices is his frequent appeal to the "ultimate authority"—God or Jesus Christ. When asked by NBC's John Bachman on December 13 of 1999 to state the political philosopher or thinker with whom he could most identify, he did not say Aristotle, Plato, J. S. Mill, or John Rawls; he said, "Christ, because he changed my heart"—a savvy answer, perhaps sincere, but also likely to curry favor with the Christian right. In the third debate with Kerry, Bush reaffirmed his conviction that his military actions in Afghanistan and Iraq were divinely sanctioned.

> I believe that *God wants everybody to be free.* That's what I believe. And that's been part of my foreign policy. In Afghanistan, I believe that the freedom there is a gift from the Almighty. And I can't tell you how encouraged I am to see freedom on the march. And so *my principles that I make decisions on are a part of me, and religion is a part of me.*

If sincere, then Bush's actions are also a form of "jihad" and he comes off no better than Osama bin Laden, who too claims to be acting at the behest of the "Almighty". If insincere, it's a clever dodge that makes challenging him on this issue difficult, because of the importance of religion to voters today.

Below, Bush appeals both to deity and Franklin Roosevelt in the State of the Union Address of 2005.

> As *Franklin Roosevelt* once reminded Americans, "Each age is a dream that is dying, or one that is coming to birth". And we live in the country where the biggest dreams are born. The abolition of slavery was only a dream—until it was fulfilled. The liberation of Europe from fascism was only a dream—until it was achieved. The fall of imperial communism was only a dream—until, one day, it was accomplished. Our generation has dreams of its own, and we also go forward with confidence. *The road of Providence is uneven and unpredictable—yet we know where it leads: It leads to freedom.*
>
> Feb. 2, 2005

In his second Inaugural address, he appeals both to Abraham Lincoln and deity to make his point:

> From the day of our Founding, we have proclaimed that every man and woman on this earth has rights, and dignity, and matchless value, because *they bear the image of the Maker of Heaven and earth....*

> The rulers of outlaw regimes can know that we still believe as *Abraham Lincoln* did: "Those who deny freedom to others deserve it not for themselves; and, *under the rule of a just God*, cannot long retain it".
>
> Inaugural Address, Jan. 20, 2005

Chapter 9
Rule IV: Express Your Confusion Unabashedly

"Alice felt dreadfully puzzled. The Hatter's remark seemed to her to have no sort of meaning in it, and yet it was certainly English. 'I don't quite understand you', she said, as politely as she could".

Finally, whenever Bush's is overly confused by a question or on an issue, he merely expresses his utter confusion, without shame, by saying something insipid or idiotic. This rule should seem utterly senseless to any rational politician. Yet this is just what makes it an effective rhetorical tool. Coming across as a buffoon throws an adversary so much off guard that this adversary becomes speechless and incapable of mounting an attack. It makes no sense for an adversary to attack you, when you have in effect already attacked yourself! Moreover, coming across to others confused—especially when one really is confused—fosters public sympathy. One has only to consider public opinion after the Bush/Gore and Bush/Kerry debates. His two democratic opponents in these two campaigns came across as snobbish intellectuals—like those book readers with whom Bush refused to associate at Yale—while Bush was lauded for "holding his own"—that is, he may have come across as a buffoon, but not a *complete* buffoon.

Drawing Obvious Conclusions

The easiest way to do this is to repeat in your conclusion the very evidence you give in support of it. One need not fear being redundant: Redundancy works. Moreover, in logic, it's legitimate—sort of. Who would think of challenging an argument such as: *It's sunny outside*, because *it's sunny outside*?

Consider the following exchange between Bush and Brit Hume on July 19 of 2000 that concerned the upcoming Republican convention.

> Hume: What if there isn't any unity at the Republican convention?
> Bush: I am confident there will be. I'm confident people are coming together. *And the reason I believe this is because our party is united.*
>
> *Fox Special Report,* July 19, 2000

In logic, this is called "circular reasoning", for obvious reasons. It is a legitimate, though undesirable, form of argument: legitimate, because if what you are arguing *from* is true, then what you are arguing *to* must be true; undesirable, because if there is any doubt concerning the truth of the conclusion, then this same doubt applies to the premise and if there is no doubt about the truth of the premise, then the conclusion is redundant.

I list some other examples, some of which are not explicitly circular, below:

> Tribal sovereignty means that, it's sovereign. You're a—you've been given sovereignty, and you're viewed as a sovereign entity. And,

therefore, the relationship between the federal government and tribes is one between sovereign entities.

Aug. 6, 2004

See, one of the interesting things in the Oval Office—I love to bring people into the Oval Office—right around the corner from here, and say, "*This is where I office [*sic*]*", but I want you to know the office is always bigger than the person.

Washington Post, Feb. 20, 2004

The reason I believe in a large tax cut, *because it's what I believe.*

More Muslims have died at the hands of killers than—I say more Muslims—a lot of Muslims have died—I don't know the exact count—at Istanbul. Look at these different places around the world where there's been tremendous death and destruction *because killers kill.*

Jan. 29, 2004

It is not Reaganesque to support a tax plan that is Clinton in nature.

Los Angeles, Feb. 23, 2000

If somebody's so calculating that they spend their whole life calculating the path to the presidency, when they become president, *they'll be calculating.*

Readers Digest UK Online, Aug. 30, 2000

Drawing Inconsistent Conclusions

On the other extreme, there are times when Bush draws conclusions that regard for right reasoning disallows. Recall these two gems on deterrence:

I'm worried about the fact that our mission is not clear. It ought to be to have a military that's properly trained and equipped to be able to fight and win war, *and, therefore, prevent war from happening in the first place.*

Nov. 3, 2000

> The mission of the military is to fight and be able to win war, and *therefore prevent war from happening in the first place.*
>
> GOP Debate, Feb. 15, 2000

One other example that is strictly not inconsistent, since it expresses Bush's belief state, not a state of external affairs, is as follows:

> I strongly support the faith-based initiative that we're proposing because *I don't believe it violates the line between the separation of church and state*. [It does.] And I believe it's going to make America a better place.
>
> *New York Times*, Feb. 23, 2001

Finally, there's this doozey to the FBI Academy:

> Free societies are peaceful societies. So, in the long run, the only way to defeat the ideologies of hatred and fear, *the only way to make sure our country is secure in the long run, is to advance the cause of freedom.*
>
> July 11, 2005

It's All Black-and-White

The black-and-white fallacy occurs when one argues by making a sharp and clear, black-and-white distinction that is given little or no support by reality. Such thinking, similar to the way a child partitions reality, is seemingly a part of the essence of Bush. Try as he might, he cannot seem to see the myriad nuances of reality. It may be, just as he said to Senator Biden, "Joe, I don't do nuance".[1]

> Every nation in every region now has a decision to make. *Either you are with us or you are with the terrorists.* From this day forward, any nation that continues to harbor or support terrorism will be regarded by the United States as a hostile regime.
>
> Sept. 20, 2001

1 *Time*, Feb. 15, 2004.

> But the best way to protect this homeland is to stay on the offense. *You know, we have to be right 100 percent of the time.* And the enemy only has to be right once to hurt us.
>
> Bush/Kerry I, Sept. 30, 2004

Here Bush addresses the United Nations not long after 9/11 in black-and-white fashion.

> As I've told the American people, freedom and fear are at war. We face enemies that hate not our policies, but our existence; the tolerance of openness and creative culture that defines us. But the outcome of this conflict is certain: There is a current in history and it runs toward freedom. Our enemies resent it and dismiss it, but the dreams of mankind are defined by liberty—the natural right to create and build and worship and live in dignity. When men and women are released from oppression and isolation, they find fulfillment and hope, and they leave poverty by the millions.
>
> Nov. 10, 2001

Next, months after 9/11, Bush explains that America was attacked by those who hate freedom simple because America is the nation that symbolizes freedom.

> And you're probably wondering, why would somebody hit us? And it's because we love freedom. There are people in the world who cannot stand a free society. There are people who do not believe that you should be able to worship freely. There are people who do not believe you should be able to speak freely. There are people who do not believe that young women should be educated. And when they find a nation that's willing to defend freedom, they try to attack it.... You know, I laid out an initiative that said *you're either with us or you're against us*; either you stand with America to defend freedom, so that you can grow up, and your children can grow up, in a society, in a civilized world that values individual freedoms. And most nations of the world chose to be with us. And for that, our nation is grateful.
>
> Mar. 4, 2002

In the United Nations' Address of 2003, Bush states that, between the order-seekers and the chaos-seekers, there is the "clearest of divides".

> Events during the past two years have set before us the clearest of divides: between *those who seek order*, and *those who spread chaos*; between *those who work for peaceful change*, and *those who adopt the methods of gangsters*; between *those who honor the rights of man* and *those who deliberately take the lives of men and women and children without mercy or shame*.
>
> *Between these alternatives there is no neutral ground.* All governments that support terror are complicit in a war against civilization. No government should ignore the threat of terror, because to look the other way gives terrorists the chance to regroup and recruit and prepare. And all nations that fight terror, as if the lives of their own people depend on it, will earn the favorable judgment of history.
>
> Sept. 23, 2003

In this recent press conference, Bush struggles with the question concerning his insistence on a diplomatic solution to the problem of North Korea's nuclear program. The military "solution", of course, is not an option, with the U.S. military being spread so thin across the globe.

> Well, then let's see—if it's the wrong—if diplomacy is the wrong approach, I guess that means military. That's how I view it—it's either diplomacy or military. And I am for the diplomacy approach. And so, for those who say that we ought to be using our military to solve the problem, I would say that, while all options are on the table, we've got—we've got a ways to go to solve this diplomatically.
>
> May 31, 2005

Other select quotes:

> The unexpected, obviously, was September the eleventh, when evil people decided to attack America. I say "evil people" because I don't view this as a religious war. *I view this as a struggle of good versus evil.* And, make no mistake about it, good will prevail.
>
> Jan. 5, 2002

> *I don't see many shades of gray in the war and terror. Either you're with us or you're against us. And it's a struggle between good and between evil.*
>
> Feb. 8, 2002

> We will persistently clarify the choice before every ruler and every nation: *The moral choice between oppression, which is always wrong, and freedom, which is eternally right.* America will not pretend that jailed dissidents prefer their chains, or that women welcome humiliation and servitude, or that any human being aspires to live at the mercy of bullies.
>
> Inaugural Address, Jan. 20, 2005

> The Iraqis want to live in a free society. Zawahiri [al-Qaeda's number two man] doesn't want them [the Iraqis] to live in a free society. And that's the clash of ideologies—freedom versus tyranny. We have had these kinds of clashes before, and we have prevailed. We have prevailed because we're right; we have prevailed because we adhere to a hopeful philosophy; and we have prevailed because we would not falter.
>
> Aug. 4, 2005

Non Sequitur

Non sequitur literally means "it does not follow". Thus, it is an argument whose conclusion does not follow from its premise(s). Here is an exchange between Larry King and Bush:

> Larry King: Only one percent of Americans are even affected by [the death tax], right"
>
> Bush: Well, if that's the case, let's do it.
>
> King: Yes, but when one percent convinces 99 percent that it's in their best interest to lower their…
>
> Bush: Well, maybe we ought—maybe we ought— I don't know the figure of one percent or 99 percent, but if that—*if it's good public policy, it's good public policy.*
>
> *Larry King Live,* CNN, July 20, 2000

> This is a world that is much more uncertain than the past. In the past, we were certain, we were certain it was us versus the Russians in the past. We were certain, and *therefore we had huge nuclear arsenals aimed at each other to keep the peace….* You see, even though it's an uncertain world, we're certain of some things.
>
> *Washington Post*, May 31, 2000

The third debate with John Kerry produced this retrodictive gem:

> My opponent said this is a bitterly divided time. Pretty divided in the 2000 election. *So in other words, it's pretty divided during the 1990s as well.*

Bush was happy to justify his pro-life stance in the following *non-sequitur.*

> My pro-life position is I believe there's life. It's not necessarily based on religion. I think there's a life there, *therefore life, liberty and pursuit of happiness.*
>
> *San Francisco Chronicle*, Jan. 23, 2001

Next, I give an exchange between Tim Russert and Bush, where Russert challenges the president's military record.

Russert:	Mr. President, this campaign is fully engaged. The chairman of the Democratic National Committee, Terence McAuliffe, said this last week: "I look forward to that debate when John Kerry, a war hero with a chest full of medals, is standing next to George Bush, a man who was AWOL in the Alabama National Guard. He didn't show up when he should have showed up—"
Bush:	Yeah.
Russert:	How do you respond?
Bush:	Political season is here. I was—I served in the National Guard. I flew F-102 aircraft. I got an honorable discharge. I've heard this—I've heard this ever since I started running for office. I—I put in my time, proudly so. I would be careful to not denigrate the Guard. It's fine to go after me, which I expect the other side will do. I wouldn't denigrate service to the Guard, though, and the reason I wouldn't, is because there are a lot of really fine people who have served in the National Guard and who are serving in the National Guard today in Iraq.
Russert:	The Boston Globe and the Associated Press have gone through some of the records and said there's no evidence that you reported to duty in Alabama during the summer and fall of 1972.
Bush:	Yeah, *they're—they're just wrong. There may be no evi-*

> *dence, but I did report; otherwise, I wouldn't have been honorably discharged.* In other words, you don't just say "I did something" without there being verification. Military doesn't work that way. I got an honorable discharge, and I did show up in Alabama.
>
> *Meet the Press*, Feb. 7, 2004

The thrust here is the notion "If I didn't report, I wouldn't have been honorably discharged" and "I was honorably discharged", so it must be the case "I did report". Yet isn't being "honorably discharged" is also consistent with "not reporting"—especially when one's father is George H. W. Bush?

This *non sequitur* has a fairly obvious premise and a fairly frightening conclusion.

> *I'm not the expert on how the Iraqi people think*, because I live in America, where it's nice and safe and secure.
>
> Sept. 23, 2004

Makes one wonder why Iraq is such a dangerous place, doesn't it?

In this recent press conference, Bush gets, for lack of a better term, conclusion-happy. Note how many conclusions he draws on Iran's violation of the NPT (Nuclear Non-Proliferation Treaty) agreement.

> Now, our policy is very clear on that, and that is that the Iranians violated the NPT agreement; we found out they violated the agreement, and, *therefore*, they're not to be trusted when it comes to highly-enriched uranium—or highly-enriching uranium. And, *therefore*, our policy is to prevent them from having the capacity to develop enriched uranium to the point where they're able to make a nuclear weapon. Secondly—*and so, therefore*, we're working with the EU-3 to hopefully convince the Iranians to abandon their pursuits of such a program. And it appears we're making some progress.
>
> May 31, 2005

In the same press conference, Bush talks about the tension between China and Taiwan and draws a conclusion that concerns the size of China! Egad once again!

> China is a—obviously, there's tension on—about Taiwan that we have to deal with. And I made my position very clear and very consistent about Taiwan. The Taiwanese understand my position; the Chinese understand my position. So, in this case, the relationship is one of helping to solve that problem, is to keeping stability in the region so that eventually there will be a peaceful solution to that issue. *And so China is a fascinating country that is significant in its size.*

Again, in this press conference, Bush argues, strangely enough, that terrorists kill as they do *precisely because they see the benefits of democracy.* Suffice it to say, this was not a very good day for the president!

> These are incredibly hopeful times—and very difficult times. And the problem is, is that I not only see the benefits of democracy, but *so do the terrorists.* And that's why they want to blow people up, indiscriminately kill, in order to shake the will of the Iraqis, or perhaps create a civil war, or to get us to withdraw early. That's what they're trying to do, because they fear democracy. *They understand what I just—they understand what I understand. There's kind of a meeting of minds on that.* And that's why the American people are seeing violent actions on their TV screens, because these people want to—the killers want us to get out. They want us to—they want the Iraqis to quit. They understand what a democracy can mean to their backward way of thinking.
>
> May 31, 2005

Finally, when asked in an interview by *The Times* of London about the U.S.'s record in Africa, Bush replied absurdly:

> We've got a great record in Africa, and the reason we've got a great record in Africa is that I believe in the admonition, "To whom much has been given, much is required".
>
> June 29, 2005

Equivocation

To equivocate is to use a word that has more than one meaning in one way in one part of an argument and in another way in another part. Below, Bush starts out talking about a single mom who makes $40,000 per year and has two children and presumably ends up talking about a single mom with two children, who [each?] make $40,000 per year!

> One of the features in my plan, John, says to the single mom with two children making $40,000 a year, you get a 53 percent tax cut. For single moms with children who make less than $40,000 a year get—get bigger tax cuts. My question to you is, in reviewing of your plan, that single mom with children—two children, making $40,000—get no tax cut. And I'm wondering why.
>
> GOP Debate, Des Moines, Dec. 13, 1999

In this quote, Bush begins by talking of governors *of states* and ends up talking of governors *as states.*

> I have been a governor *of* a big state, I have made education my number one priority. That's what governors ought to do. They ought to say this is the most important thing we do *as* a state.
>
> Bush-Gore III, Oct. 17, 2000

Finally, note the dexterous use of the word "it" below in a question about the attitude that the U.S. should have concerning China.

> I think that we ought—it is a—the relationship with China is a very complex relationship, and Americans ought to view it as such. China is a emerging nation. It's an amazing story to watch here. I mean, it's consuming more and more natural resources; it is generating jobs and exporting a lot of goods; it's a massive market.
>
> May 31, 2005

SECTION FOUR
PROPOSITIONALLY CHALLENGED PRESIDENT

> "I'm also not very analytical. You know I don't spend a lot of time thinking about myself, about why I do things".
>
> George W. Bush

THE FIRST THREE SECTIONS WERE A LOOK at Bush's unique looking-glass logic through his political and ethical reasoning as well as the various rhetorical devices that he both consciously and unconsciously uses in addresses, press conferences, interviews, and, at times, casual conversations.

The use of logic in everyday reasoning, however, presupposes a prior capacity to string together sentences properly—something learned in our formative years and reinforced throughout the educative stage of our life.

This final chapter has a simple, but ambitious aim. I hope to show that one of the main reasons the president of the United States cannot reason properly is that he has great difficulty stringing together sentences properly. From the perspective of logic, Bush is propositionally challenged. This, final chapter, then, is an often amusing, A-to-Z look the various ways Bush uses and *misuses* sentences. Commentary throughout will be minimal. I wish to let Bush himself speak to his own confusion with words.

Chapter 10
Bush: A to F

"'But "glory" doesn't mean "a nice knock-down argument"', Alice objected. 'When I use a word', Humpty Dumpty said in rather a scornful tone, 'it means just what I choose it to mean—neither more nor less'.

"'The question is', said Alice, 'whether you can make words means o many different things'.

"'The question is', said Humpty Dumpty, 'which is to be master—that's all'".

Choice Absurdities

I begin this chapter with a sample of various absurd claims that Bush had made throughout the years.

> I mean, there needs to be wholesale effort against racial profiling, which is illiterate children.
>
> Bush/Gore II, Oct. 11, 2000

> Drug therapies are replacing a lot of medicines as we used to know it.
>
> Bush/Gore III, Oct. 17, 2000

Redefining the role of the United States from enablers to keep the peace to enablers to keep the peace from peacekeepers is going to be an assignment.

Jan. 14, 2001

This administration is doing everything we can to end the stalemate in an efficient way. We're making the right decisions to bring the solution to an end.

April 10, 2001

Can't living with the bill [McCain-Kennedy patient's bill] means it won't become law.

June 13, 2001

You know, sometimes when you study history, you get stuck in the past.

Wall Street Journal, June 25, 2001

We are fully committed to working with both sides to bring the level of terror down to an acceptable level for both.

Oct. 2, 2001

We hold dear what our Declaration of Independence says, that all have got uninalienable [*sic*] rights, endowed [*sic*] by a Creator.

Moscow, May 24, 2002

I'm thrilled to be here in the bread basket of America because it gives me a chance to remind our fellow citizens that we have an advantage here in America—we can feed ourselves.

Stockton, CA, Aug. 23, 2002

President Musharraf, he's still tight with us on the war against terror, and that's what I appreciate. He's a—he understands that we've got to keep Al Qaeda on the run, and that by keeping him [*sic*] on the run, it's more likely we will bring him to justice.

Ruch, OR, Aug. 22, 2002

There's no cave deep enough for America, or dark enough to hide.

Oklahoma City, Aug. 29, 2002

Any time we've got any kind of inkling that somebody is thinking about doing something to an American and something to our homeland, you've just got to know we're moving on it, to protect the United Nations Constitution, and at the same time, we're protecting you.

Aberdeen, SD, Oct. 31, 2002

The war on terror involves Saddam Hussein because of the nature of Saddam Hussein, the history of Saddam Hussein, and his willingness to terrorize himself.

Grand Rapids, MI, Jan. 29, 2003

We ended the rule of one of history's worst tyrants, and in so doing, we not only freed the American people, we made our own people more secure.

Crawford, TX, May 3, 2003

I think war is a dangerous place.

May 7, 2003

As Luce reminded me, he said, without data, without facts, without information, the discussions about public education mean that a person is just another opinion.

Jacksonville, Sept. 9, 2003

Well, I think in my speech on the Abraham Lincoln, if they looked at the words [*sic*], I said, "It's still a dangerous place".

Interview with Brit Hume, Sept. 22, 2003

I'm honored to shake the hand of a brave Iraqi citizen who had his hand cut off by Saddam Hussein.

May 25, 2004

Too many good docs are getting out of the business. Too many OB/GYN's aren't able to practice their love with women all across the country.

Poplar Bluff, MO, Sept. 6, 2004

Blatant Self-Contradictions

The mission of the military is to fight and be able to win war, and therefore prevent war from happening in the first place.

GOP Debate, Feb. 15, 2000

I did denounce it. I de—I denounced it. I denounced interracial dating. I denounced anti-Catholic bigacy [sic]—bigotry. No, I—I—I—I spoke out against interracial dating. I mean, I support inter—the policy of interracial dating.

CBS Evening News, Feb. 25, 2000

The fact that [Gore] relies on facts—says things that are not factual—are [*sic*] going to undermine his campaign.

New York Times, Mar. 4, 2000

Unfairly but truthfully, our party has been tagged as being against things. Anti-immigration, for example. And we're not a party of anti-immigrants. Quite the opposite. We're a party that welcomes people.

July 1, 2000

King: One of the things [Gore] said is you're the forty-fifth—thirty-seventh in per capita spending on education in America. That's pretty low for a state that big.

Bush: You know, he's critical of everything. I mean, this is a campaign really where he'll tear down every single aspect of what is a very positive record. And you know, he may want to look at it—I mean, listen, *you can talk about numbers all the time*, but *what matters are results*. And we lead the nation when it comes to improvement. Say, for example, amongst minority students, *Texas and North Carolina are ranked the two best* when it comes to improving in test scores for Hispanic youngsters or African-American youngsters.

Larry King Live, CNN, July 20, 2000

One of the reasons I came to this school was because I love to highlight beacons of hope, centers of excellence that challenge the odds. One of the common denominators I have found is that expectations rise above that which is expected.

Los Angeles, Sept. 27, 2000

There's no such thing as legacies. At least, there is a legacy, but I'll never see it.

Jan. 31, 2001

Education is not my top priority. Applause. Education is my top priority.

Feb. 27, 2001

I'm sure you can imagine it's an unimaginable honor to live here [in the White House].

June 18, 2001

See, free nations are peaceful nations. Free nations don't attack each other. Free nations don't develop weapons of mass destruction.

Milwaukee, Oct. 3, 2003

I cut the taxes on everybody. I didn't cut them. The Congress cut them. I asked them to cut them.

Aug. 6, 2004

After standing on the stage, after the debates, I made it very plain, we will not have an all-volunteer army. And yet, this week—we will have an all-volunteer army. Let me restate that.

Daytona Beach, Fla., Oct. 16, 2004

Queer Conditionals

Well, I think if you say you're going to do something and don't do it, that's trustworthiness.

CNN Online Chat, Aug. 30, 2000

If you're sick and tired of the politics of cynicism and polls and principles, come and join this campaign.

Hilton Heard, SC, Feb. 16, 2000

The culture of my generation, our generation, has clearly said, "If it feels good, do it, and be sure to blame somebody else if you have a problem".

Vanity Fair, Oct., 2000

If a person doesn't have the capacity that we all want that person to have, I suspect hope is in the far distant future, if at all.

May 22, 2001

If you can make 50 cents in the heart of Mexico, for example, or make $5 here in America, $5—15, you're going to come here if you're worth your salt, if you want to put food on the table for your families.

Bush/Gore III, Oct. 17, 2004

> I know it is in the interest of the Palestinian people that they can live in—a society in which they can realize their dreams if they happen to be an entrepreneur.
>
> Nov. 12, 2004

> [W]hen you engage the terrorists abroad, it causes activity and action.
>
> Apr. 28, 2005

It's All about Dubya

> Actually, I—this may sound a little West Texan to you, but I like it. When I'm talking about—when I'm talking about myself, and when he's talking about myself, all of us are talking about me.
>
> *Hardball*, MSNBC, May 31, 2000

> I have a proud record of working with both Republicans and Democrats, which is what our nation needs. Somebody that can come to Washington and say let's forget all the finger pointing and get positive things done on Medicare, prescription drugs, Social Security, and so I take him for his word.
>
> Bush/Gore I, Oct. 3, 2000

> This is an impressive crowd, the haves and the have-mores. Some people call you the elite. I call you my base.
>
> Al Smith Memorial Dinner in New York, Oct. 19, 2000

> It's amazing I won. I was running against peace, prosperity, and incumbency.
>
> June 14, 2001

> I know what I believe. I will continue to articulate what I believe and what I believe—I believe what I believe is right.
>
> Rome, July 22, 2001

Often times, as in the next two examples below, Bush's comments about others or other countries seem equally applicable to himself and America.

> They love only one thing. They love power, and when they have it, they use it without mercy.
>
> Charleston, SC, Dec. 11, 2001

I worry about a regime that is closed and not transparent.

Feb. 20, 2002

The following remark, in an attempt to sum his first year as president, came just a few months after 9/11! The comment shows profound indifference to the suffering of a nation.

But all in all, it's been a fabulous year for Laura and me.

Dec. 21, 2001

Laura and I will thank them from the bottom of my heart.

Alexandria, Virginia, March 20, 2002

Sometimes when I sleep at night I think of [Dr. Seuss's] *Hop on Pop*.

Apr. 2, 2002

I try to go for longer runs, but it's tough around here at the White House on the outdoor track. It's sad that I can't run longer. It's one of the saddest things about the presidency.

Aug. 21, 2002

There's only one person who hugs the mothers and the widows, the wives and the kids upon the death of their loved one. Others hug, but having committed the troops, I've got an additional responsibility to hug and that's me and I know what it's like.

Dec. 11, 2002

I glance at the headlines just to kind-of get a flavor for what's moving. I rarely read the stories, and get briefed by people who are probably read [*sic*] the news themselves.

Interview with Brit Hume, Sept. 22, 2003

I'm not telling [about picks for the Supreme Court]. I really don't have—haven't picked anybody yet. Plus, *I want them all voting for me.*

Bush/Kerry II, Oct. 8, 2004

And I think when the people take a look at my government, they'll say, "Gosh, that ol' George W. is surrounding himself with some great people". And I have. And I give them a chance to tell me what's on their mind. I listen carefully, and then I make up my mind, and they say, "Yes, sir, Mr. President".

Danish Broadcasting Corp., June 29, 2005

M. Andrew Holowchak

Educational "Bloopers"

Higher education is not [*sic*] my priority.

San Antonio Express-News, Mar. 22, 1998

What's not fine is, rarely is the question asked, "Are—is our children [*sic*] learning?"

Los Angeles Times, Jan. 14, 2000

How do you know, if you don't measure—if you have a system that simply suckles [*sic*] kids through?

Beaufort, SC, Feb. 16, 2000

I want it to be said that the Bush administration was a results-oriented administration, because I believe the results of focusing our attention and energy on teaching children to read and having an education system that's responsive to the child and to the parents, as opposed to mired in a system that refuses to change, will make America what we want it to be—a more literate country and a hopefuller [*sic*] country.

Jan. 11, 2001

You teach a child to read, and he or she will be able to pass a literacy test.

Townsend, TN, Feb. 21, 2001

We must have the attitude that every child in America—regardless of where they're raised or how they're born—can learn.

New Britain, CT, Apr. 18, 2001

The public education system in America is one of the most important foundations of our democracy. After all, it is where children from all over America learn to be responsible citizens, and learn to have the skills necessary to take advantage of our fantastic opportunistic [*sic*] society.

May 1, 2002

And if you're interested in the quality of education and you're paying attention to what you hear at Laclede, why don't you volunteer? Why don't you mentor a child how to read [*sic*]?

St. Louis, Jan. 5, 2004

I'm so Flummoxed!

Bush: I talked with my little brother, Jeb—I haven't told this to many people. But he's the governor of—I shouldn't call him my little brother—my brother, Jeb, the great governor of Texas—

Lehrer: Florida.

Bush: Florida. The state of Florida.

Interview with Jim Lehrer, Apr. 27, 2000

I suspect that had my dad not been president, he'd be asking the same questions: "How'd your meeting go with so-and-so?" "How did you feel when you stood up in front of the people for the State of the Union Address—State of the Budget Address?"—whatever you call it.

Washington Post, Mar. 9, 2001

Question: Mr. President, what's your reaction to the new bin Laden tape this week? And do you fear he's now alluded the manhunt? Also, are you concerned that if military tribunals require a unanimous verdict for the death penalty, some terrorists could avoid execution?

Bush: Let me start with the first of your three questions. Which was what? I've already forgotten.

Crawford, TX, Dec. 28, 2001

Question: Mr. President, you expressed confidence in the Prime Minister again today. But he's been in office for about a year now, and he's been unable to enact structural reforms. Why do you think it's taken so long for the Japanese government to enact the reforms you're talking about? And to the Prime Minister, you called the President's alternative to Kyoto a positive proposal. That given, do you think the world's environment would have been better off if America had signed on to Kyoto?

Bush: The second question is moot. What was the first question?

Question: Why has it taken—

Bush: Oh, that's right, yes. Listen—

Tokyo, Feb. 18, 2002

Bush:	I'm jet lagged—what's the first couple of questions.
Reporter:	The second one, sir, was I was wondering if the escalating conflict posed a threat to U.S. forces in the region.
Bush:	I would certainly hope not. Third? Is that it? (Yucks.)
Reporter:	Memorial Day.
Bush:	Oh, Memorial Day. Thanks. That's what happens when you're over 55. (Yucks.) You know what I mean. Let me say one quick thing about Memorial Day.

Paris, May 26, 2002

> I urge the leaders in Europe and around the world to take swift, decisive action against terror groups such as Hamas, to cut off their funding, and to support—cut funding and support, as the United States has done.
>
> June 25, 2003

> I wish you'd have given me this written question [about the biggest mistake Bush has made after 9/11] ahead of time so I could plan for it. John, I'm sure historians will look back and say, gosh, he could've done it better this way or that way. You know, I just—I'm sure something will pop into my head here in the midst of this press conference, with all the pressure of trying to come up with answer, but it hadn't yet.
>
> Apr. 13, 2004

> In terms of timetables, as quickly as possible—whatever that means.
>
> Mar. 16, 2005

> That's part of a healthy and a peaceful—peaceful world, will be a world in which governments do respect people's rights.
>
> May 31, 2005

In the same press conference—an especially troublesome one for this verbal valetudinarian—Bush is asked a question about how he would go about selecting the next Supreme Court justice.

> Now, in terms of whether that agreement means that a senator [*sic*] is going to get an up or down vote, I guess it was vague enough for people to interpret the agreement the way they want to interpret it.
>
> May 31, 2005

It is not clear from the context what "agreement" Bush means, but the prior sentences are about consulting with the Senate.

Speaking on how to win the war on terrorism, Bush stated:

> We're going to—this is where you win the war on terror—is you go to the battlefield and you take them on. And that's what they've done.
>
> June 29, 2005

Chapter 11
Bush G to L

> *"'Curiouser and curiouser!' cried Alice (she was so much surprised, that for the moment she quite forgot how to speak good English)".*

Grammar 101

Bush's difficulties with the English language have been well documented over the years. Of especial note is his inability to link the right verb to a particular subject. Instances of this particular grammatical "infelicity" could alone fill this chapter.

> Laura and I really don't realize how bright our children is [*sic*] sometimes until we get an objective analysis.
>
> *Meet the Press*, CNBC, Apr. 15, 2000

> Strong relations in Europe is [*sic*] in our nation's interest.
>
> Bush/Gore II, Oct. 11, 2000

> Just remember it's the birds [*sic*] that's supposed to suffer, not the hunter.
>
> Roswell, N.M., Jan. 22, 2004

Then you wake up at the high-school level and find out that the illiteracy level of our children are [*sic*] appalling.

Jan. 23, 2004

I call [the U.N.'s role] a vital role because there is a lot of roles [*sic*] being played by different players, but the U.N. will play—and this role is a very important role.

Meet the Press, Feb. 7, 2004

This has been tough weeks [*sic*] in that country [Iraq'.

Apr. 13, 2004

We all thought there was [*sic*] weapons there, Robin. My opponent thought there was weapons [*sic*] there. That's why he called him a grave threat. I wasn't happy when we found out there wasn't weapons [*sic*]....

Bush/Kerry II, Oct. 8, 2004

I understand there's great differences [*sic*] on this issue of abortion....

Bush/Kerry III, Oct. 13, 2004

But there's progress being made, and so it's kind of hard to have a summary because there's different countries [*sic*], different places.

Feb. 17, 2005

As I campaigned across this country last year, the judges was [*sic*] an issue that I raised at every single stop.

Mar. 15, 2005

But Iraq has—have [*sic;* had it right the first time!] got people there that are willing to kill, and they're hard-nosed killers.

Apr. 28, 2005

There's some interesting ideas, [*sic*], that have been proposed.

May 31, 2005

And then there are those tricky prepositions....

In terms of being a president that says there's no place in racism [*sic*], it starts with saying there's no place for racism in America.

GOP Debate, Jan. 10, 2000

> I don't know about that, but yes, I think the president can call upon [*sic*] racial reconciliation in America.
>
> *Larry King Live,* CNN, Sept. 26, 2000

> And I—it's—I'm a proud man to be [missing an "in"?] the nation based upon such wonderful values.
>
> July 2, 2001

> Driving into [*sic*] the high school here, I saw a sign that said, "Thanks for the $600 rebate check".
>
> Independence, MO, Aug. 21, 2001

Here it's not merely a matter of choosing the right preposition. The words unfortunately get a bit twisted.

> As a result of securing ourselves and ridding the Taliban out of Afghanistan [ridding Afghanistan of the Taliban], the Afghan people had elections this weekend.
>
> Oct. 13, 2004

And, of course, if you don't quite know which preposition to use, try both of them.

> I was comfortable with the people by the people [*sic*] around me there, out there in Maryland.
>
> May 31, 2005

> China is a—obviously, there's tension on—about [*sic*] Taiwan that we have to deal with.
>
> May 31, 2005

And then there are those pesky articles:

> We've got people working hard in intelligence gathering around the world to get as good an information [*sic*] as possible.
>
> *Meet the Press*, Feb. 7, 2004

> I believe that I have a obligation [*sic*] to put forth good, honorable people to serve on the bench, and have done so. And I expect them to get a up or down vote on the floor of the Senate.
>
> Mar. 16, 2005

> China is a [*sic*] emerging nation.
>
> May 31, 2005

Below I list just a few other grammatical difficulties:

> Because this nation will defend ourselves [*sic*] and freedom at any price.
>
> Mar. 4, 2002

> There may be some tough times here in America. But this country was gone through [*sic*] tough times before, and we're going to do it again.
>
> Waco, TX, Aug. 13, 2002

> My six years as governor of Texas have been invaluable to me as I carry out my duties as [*sic*] the presidency.
>
> Feb. 27, 2005

> I recognize some in Congress wished I hadn't have [*sic*], brought the issue up.
>
> May 31, 2005

> So the culture of life is more than just an issue like embryonic stem cell; it's promoting a culture that is mindful that we can help—to help [had it right the first time!] save lives through compassion.
>
> May 31, 2005

> So, in this case, the relationship is one of helping to solve that problem, is to keeping [*sic*] stability in the region so that eventually there will be a peaceful solution to that issue.
>
> May 31, 2005

Oh, the Hypocrisy!

Bush's inability to empathize has been amply confirmed in recent literature and I've talked of his sadism in chapter five. Thus, the quotes below are blatantly hypocritical.

We are in a fight for our principles, and our first responsibility is to live by them.

Sept. 20, 2001

It's important to have people [like John Thune] who see the world the way it is, not the way we hope it is.

Nov. 3, 2002

See, we love—we love freedom. That's what they [the terrorists] didn't understand. They hate things; we love things. They act out of hatred; we don't seek revenge, we seek justice out of love.

Oklahoma City, Aug. 29, 2002

Our deepest national conviction is that every life is precious, because every life is the gift of a Creator who intended us to live in liberty and equality. More than anything else, this separates us from the enemy we fight. We value every life; our enemies value none—not even the innocent, not even their own. And we seek the freedom and opportunity that give meaning and value to life.

New York, Sept. 11, 2002

Hume: From a military point of view, do you regard that [the war in Iraq] as a welcome or unwelcome development?

Bush: That's an interesting question, because you know I'm a man of peace.

Interview with Brit Hume, Sept. 22, 2003

See, free societies are societies that don't develop weapons of mass terror and don't blackmail the world.

Meet the Press, Feb. 7, 2004

I've always believed that the—obviously, the best way to solve any difficult issue is through diplomacy. And in this case, France, Great Britain and Germany are handling the negotiations on behalf of the rest of the world, which is [*sic*] those nations which are deeply concerned about Iran having a nuclear weapon.

May 31, 2005

Oh, the Insincerity!

[Y]ou need somebody in office who will tell the truth.

Bush/Gore III, Oct. 17, 2000

Nobody grieves harder than I do when we lose a life. I feel responsible for sending the troops into harm's way. It breaks my heart when I see a mom sitting on the front row of a speech and she's weeping, openly weeping, for the loss of her son. I'm not very good about concealing my emotions.

Mar. 13, 2002

My attitude is—and I know John shares this with me—any time any of hurt, we all hurt. Any time somebody suffers, society suffers.

Nov. 3, 2002

And many Americans also understand what I know to be true: free societies are peaceful societies. And that's why I will continue to promote what I would call an "active foreign policy".

Interview with Brit Hume, Sept. 22, 2003

As we work for peace, other countries must step up to their reponsibilities.

May 26, 2005

For the past four years I've called on Congress to pass legislation that encourages energy conservation; that promotes domestic production in environmentally friendly ways; that helps diversify away from foreign oil; that modernizes the electricity grid; that's got a substantial amount of research and development money to help us transition from the hydrocarbon economy to a diversified source of energy economy.

May 31, 2005

Dubya's Jargon

I've coined new words, like, "misunderstanding" [*sic*] and "Hispanically".

Mar. 29, 2001

One of the interesting initiatives we've taken in Washington, D.C., is we've got these vampire-busting devices. A "vampire" is a—a cell deal you can plug in the wall to charge your cell phone.

Denver, Aug. 14, 2001

"Arbolist"—look up the word. I don't know, maybe I made it up. Anyway, it's an arbo-tree-ist somebody who knows about trees.

USA Today, Aug. 21, 2001

I just want you to know that, when we talk about war, we're really talking about peace.

June 18, 2002

The federal government and the state government must not fear programs who [*sic*] change lives, but must welcome those faith-based programs for the embetterment [*sic*] of mankind.

Stockton, Calif., Aug. 23, 2002

Let me tell you my thoughts about tax relief. When your economy is kind of ooching along, it's important to let people have more of their own money.

Boston, Oct. 4, 2002

You've also got to measure in order to begin to effect change that's just more—when there's more than talk, there's just actual—a paradigm shift.

July 1, 2003

Washington is a town where there's [*sic*] all kinds of allegations. You've heard much of the allegations. And if people have got solid information, please come forward with it. And that would be people inside the information [*sic*] who are the so-called "anonymous sources", or people outside the information—outside the administration.

Chicago, Sept. 30, 2003

[W]e've had leaks out of the administrative branch, had leaks out of the legislative branch, and out of the executive branch and the legislative branch, and I've spoken out consistently against them, and I want to know who the leakers are.

Chicago, Sept. 30, 2003

> I think the hearings will show that the Patriot Act is an important change in the law that will allow the FBI and the CIA to better share information together. We were kind of stovepiped—I guess is a way to describe it. There was—you know—kind of departments [*sic*] that at times didn't communicate—because of law, in the FBI's case.
>
> Apr. 13, 2004

> I'm going to use a fancy word "disaggregated results".
>
> Sept. 27, 2004

In these lines, Bush expresses his disappointment with Kerry's interpretation of his views on bin Laden in Leave-It-to-Beaver fashion:

> Gosh, I just don't think I ever said I'm not worried about Osama bin Laden. It's kind-of one of those exaggerations.
>
> Bush/Kerry III, Oct. 13, 2004

> I speak plainly sometimes, but you've got to be mindful of the consequences of the words. So put that down. I don't know if you'd call that a confession, a regret—something.
>
> Jan. 14, 2005

> But I view my role as the President as somebody who puts problems on the table and then calls people together to solve them.
>
> May 31, 2005

Presidential Knack

It's not enough for a president to do the job that he has to do it with efficiency, style, and competence; he has to have a knack for the job. These quotes, if anything, show that Bush has a kind-of knack for the job.

> Yesterday I met with the Russian foreign minister and when he left the meeting, he kindly said this is a man who—I'm going to paraphrase him and you need to check the facts—but—*sophisticated thinker* [egad!] We had a great discussion about foreign policy and about our relations with Russia.
>
> Interview with Jim Lehrer, Apr. 27, 2000

I don't feel like I've got all that much too important to say [*sic*] on the kind of big national issues.

20/20, Sept. 15, 2000

I've been a person that had been called a uniter, not a divider, because I accept other people's points of view.

Bush/Gore Debate II, Oct. 11, 2000

They misunderestimated [*sic*] me.

Bentonville, AR, Nov. 6, 2000

My plan reduces the national debt, and fast. So fast, in fact, that economists worry that we're going to run out of debt to retire.

Feb. 24, 2001

It is time to set aside the old partisan bickering and finger-pointing and name-calling that comes [*sic*] from freeing parents to make different choices for their children.

Apr. 12, 2001

When I take action, I'm not going to fire a $2 million missile at a $10 empty tent and hit a camel in the butt. It's going to be decisive.

Sept. 19, 2001

And one of the things we've got to make sure that we do is anything.

May 7, 2002

I was proud the other day when both Republicans and Democrats stood with me in the Rose Garden to announce their support for a clear statement of purpose for Saddam: you disarm, or we will.

Manchester, NH, Oct. 5, 2002

I need to be able to move the right people to the right place at the right time to protect you, and I'm not going to accept a lousy bill out of the United Nations Senate.

South Bend, IN, Oct. 31, 2002

I know something about being a government. And you've got a good one.

Bentonville, AR, Nov. 4, 2002

I don't bring God into my life to—to, you know, kind-of be a political person.

With Tom Brokaw, aboard Air Force One, Apr. 24, 2003

I recently met with the finance minister of the Palestinian Authority — was very impressed by his grasp of finances.

May 29, 2003

I'm the master of low expectations.

June 4, 2003

Our country puts $1 billion a year up to help feed the hungry. And we're by far the most generous nation in the world when it comes to that, and I'm proud to report that. This isn't a contest of who's the most generous. I'm just telling you as an aside. We're generous. We shouldn't be bragging about it. But we are. We're very generous.

July 16, 2003

We had a good Cabinet meeting, talked about a lot of issues. Secretary of State and Defense brought us up to date about our desires to spread freedom and peace around the world.

Aug. 1, 2003

I'm a follower of American politics.

Crawford, TX, Aug. 8, 2003

I think it's very important for the American President to mean what he says. That's why I understand that the enemy could misread what I say. That's why I try to be as clearly I can.

Sept. 23, 2004

And we've—he's [John Bolton] been through hearings and questions and questionnaires [*sic*].

May 31, 2005

And I'm looking forward to a good night's sleep on the soil of a friend.

Danish Broadcasting Corp., June 29, 2005

The best place for the facts to be done is by somebody [*sic*] who's spending time investigating it.

July 18, 2005

Let Me Be Perfectly Clear...

I think it's important for those of us in a position of responsibility to be firm in sharing our experiences, to understand that the babies out of wedlock is [*sic*] a very difficult chore for mom and baby alike—I believe we ought to say there is a different alternative than the culture that is proposed by people like Miss Wolf in society—and, you know, hopefully, condoms will work, but it [*sic*] hasn't worked.

Meet the Press, Nov. 21, 1999

What I am against is quotas. I am against hard quotas, quotas they basically delineate based upon whatever. However they delineate, quotas, I think they vulcanize society.

San Francisco Chronicle, Jan. 21, 2000

I brought this up recently with the newly elected president in Mexico. He's a man I know from Mexico.

Bush/Gore I, Oct. 3, 2000

I have said that the sanction regime is like Swiss cheese—that meant that they weren't very effective.

Feb. 22, 2001

But the true threats to stability and peace are these nations that are not very transparent, that hide behind the—that don't let people in to take a look and see what they're up to. They're very kind of authoritarian regimes. The true threat is whether or not one of these people decide, peak of anger, try to hold us hostage, ourselves; the Israelis, for example, to whom [*sic*] we'll defend, offer our defenses; the South Koreans.

Mar. 13, 2001

I'm a patient man. And when I say I'm a patient man, I mean I'm a patient man. Nothing he [Saddam Hussein] has done has convinced me—I'm confident the Secretary of Defense—that he is the kind of fellow that is willing to forgo weapons of mass destruction, is willing to be a peaceful neighbor, that is—will honor the people—the Iraqi people of all stripes, will—values human life. He hasn't convinced me, nor has he convinced my administration.

Crawford, TX, Aug. 21, 2002

People say, "How can I help on this war against terror? How can I fight evil?" You can do so by mentoring a child—by going into a shut-in's house and say, "I love you".

Sept. 19, 2002

[T]he best way to find these terrorists who hide in holes is to get people coming forth to describe the location of the hole, is to give clues and data.

Dec. 15, 2003

I'm so pleased to be able to say hello to Bill Scranton. He's one of the great Pennsylvania political families.

Sept. 15, 2003

The march to war affected the people's confidence. It's hard to make investment. See, if you're a small business owner or a large business owner and you're thinking about investing, you've got to be optimistic when you invest. Except when you're marching to war, it's not a very optimistic thought, is it? In other words, it's the opposite of optimistic when you're thinking you're going to war.

Springfield, MO., Feb. 9, 2004

"Recession" means that people's incomes, at the employer level, are going down, basically, relative to costs—people are getting laid off.

Feb. 19, 2004

"Tribal sovereignty" means that, it's sovereign. You're a—you've been given sovereignty, and you're viewed as a sovereign entity.

Aug. 6, 2004

So community colleges are accessible, they're available, they're affordable, and their curriculums don't get stuck. In other words, if there's a need for a certain kind of worker, I presume your curriculums evolved over time.

Niceville, Fla., Aug. 10, 2004

We deal with threats before they fully materialize. What that means is that in the old days you could see a threat, and you may deal with it or you may not deal with it, but you never thought a threat would come to harm us. Those days are gone.

Interview with Rush Limbaugh, Aug. 31, 2004

> For some, September the 11th was a passing moment in history. In other words, it was a terrible moment, but it passes.
>
> Mainz, Germany, Feb. 23, 2005

> I was amazed by the report the other day that there is some $330 billion a year that goes unpaid by American taxpayers. It's a phenomenal amount of money. To me, it screams for making the tax system easier to understand, more fair [*sic*] and to make sure that people pay their taxes—"more fair" means pay what you owe.
>
> Apr. 28, 2005

> My position on that issue is very clear, and has been clear, about the occupation [Soviet occupation of the Baltic states]. And the position of my country has been clear about the occupation, ever since the occupation took place.
>
> Riga, Latvia, May 7, 2005

Oftentimes, Bush clarifies himself when there is no need of clarification—that is, when clarification becomes redundancy—somthing commonly found in children who learn a new word.

> I view our nuclear arsenal as a deterrent; as a way to say to people that would harm America: "Don't do it". That's a deterrent—that there is a consequence.
>
> Mar. 13, 2002

> Now, we talked to Joan Hanover. She and her husband, George, were visiting with us. They are near retirement—retiring—in the process of retiring, meaning they're very smart, active, capable people who are retirement age and are retiring.
>
> Alexandria, Va., Feb. 12, 2003

These clarifying remarks in Tampa are enough to force a recovering alcoholic to reconsider taking a belt!

> Because the—all which is on the table begins to address the big cost drivers. For example, how benefits are calculate, for example, is on the table; whether or not benefits rise based upon wage increases or price increases. There's a series of parts of the formula that are being considered. And when you couple that, those different cost drivers, affecting those—changing those with personal accounts, the idea is to get what

has been promised more likely to be—or closer delivered to what has been promised. Does that make any sense to you? It's kind of muddled. Look, there's a series of things that cause the—like, for example, benefits are calculated based upon the increase of wages, as opposed to the increase of prices. Some have suggested that we calculate—the benefits will rise based upon inflation, as opposed to wage increases. There is a reform that would help solve the red if that were put into effect. In other words, how fast benefits grow, how fast the promised benefits grow, if those—if that growth is affected, it will help on the red.

Tampa, FL, Feb. 4, 2005

We proposed a plan that takes the—solving the issue about solvency farther down the road than any other President has proposed. In other words, we're putting ideas out.

May 31, 2005

So this [the Social Security issue] is—this is a process here, and in that you love to follow the process, I will give you some insight into what I think is going to happen in the process. It's just going—it's like water cutting through a rock. It's just a matter of time. We're just going to keep working and working and working, reminding the American people that we have a serious problem and a great opportunity to act, not as politicians, but as statesmen and women to solve a problem.

May 31, 2005

And people who went and analyzed the situation [the inspectors in Iraq] came back and said, "Look, he was a dangerous person—even though no weapons were found, the ability to make weapons, and his intent and his relationship with terrorists".

Danish Broadcasting Corp., June 29, 2005

Chapter 12
Bush: M to R

"'[E]verybody that hears me sing it—either it brings the tears into their eyes, or else—'

"'Or else what?' said Alice, for the Knight had made a sudden pause. "'Or else it doesn't, you know...'".

Malaproprisms

It was just inebriating [*sic*] what Midland was all about then.

First Son, 1994

Other Republican candidates may retort [*sic*] to personal attacks and negative ads.

Washington Post, Mar. 24, 2000

We cannot let terrorists and rogue nations hold this nation hostile or hold our allies hostile [*sic*].

Iowa, Aug. 21, 2000

The point is, this is a way to help inoculate [*sic*] me about what has come and is coming.

New York Times, Sept. 2, 2000

A tax cut is really one of the anecdotes [*sic*] to coming out of an economic illness.

The Edge with Paula Zahn, Sept. 18, 2000

But it's important to have credibility and credibility is formed by being strong with your friends and resoluting [*sic*] your determination.

Bush/Gore Debate II, Oct. 11, 2000

I don't want nations feeling like that they can bully ourselves [*sic*] and our allies. I want to have a ballistic defense system so that we can make the world more peaceful, and at the same time I want to reduce our own nuclear capacities to the level commiserate [*sic*] with keeping the peace.

Des Moines, IA, Oct. 23, 2000

We're freeing women and children from incredible impression [*sic*].

Aurora, MO, Jan., 14, 2002

That's why I told President Putin and told the country, if need be, we'll just reduce unilaterally to a level commiserate [*sic*] with keeping a deterrence and keeping the peace.

Mar. 13, 2002

John Thune has got a common-sense vision for good forest policy. I look forward to working with him in the United Nations Senate [*sic*] to preserve these national heritages.

Aberdeen, SD, Oct. 31, 2002

The law I sign today directs new funds and new focus to the task of collecting vital intelligence on terrorist threats and on weapons of mass production [*sic*].

Nov. 27, 2002

We've got hundreds of sites to exploit [*sic*], looking for the chemical and biological weapons that we know Saddam Hussein had prior to our entrance into Iraq.

Santa Clara, CA, May 2, 2003

Oftentimes, we live in a processed [*sic*] world—you know, people focus on the process and not results.

May 29, 2003

And the other lesson is that there are people who can't stand what America stands for, and desire to conflict [*sic*] great harm on the American people.

Pittsburgh, July 28, 2003

I want to remind you all that in order to fight and win the war, it requires an expenditure of money that is commiserate [*sic*] with keeping a promise to our troops to make sure that they're well-paid, well-trained, well-equipped.

Dec. 15, 2003

Like you, I have been disgraced [*sic*] about what I've seen on TV that took place in prison.

Parkersburg, WV, May 13, 2004

They can get in line like those who have been here legally and have been working to become a citizenship [*sic*] in a legal manner.

Dec. 20, 2004

We have enough coal to last for 250 years, yet coal also prevents [*sic*] an environmental challenge.

Apr. 20, 2005

I subscribe that—this may be controversial for some—I subscribe [*sic*] it [that Bush sleeps well at night] to the fact that I've got peace of mind.

Danish Broadcasting Corp., June 29, 2005

Non-Stop Nonsense

For those that are uninsured, many of the uninsured are able-bodied, capable people capable of buying insurance choose not to do so.

WMUR, Manchester, NH, Nov. 10, 1999

We'll let our friends be the peacekeepers and the great country called America will be the pacemakers.

Houston, Sept. 6, 2000

That woman who knew I had dyslexia—I never interviewed her.

New York Times, Sept. 16, 2000

I will have a foreign-handed foreign policy.

Redwood, CA, Sept. 27, 2000

Now, the difference in our [health-care reform] plans is, I want that $2,000 to go to you, and the Vice-President [Gore] would like to be spending the $2000 on your behalf.

Bush/Gore I, Oct. 3, 2000

It's your money. You paid for it.

Lacrosse, WI, Oct. 18, 2000

Natural gas is hemispheric. I like to call it hemispheric in nature because it is a product that we can find in our neighborhoods.

Austin, Dec. 20, 2000

I think it's very important for world leaders to understand that when a new administration comes in, the new administration will be running the foreign policy.

USA Today, Jan. 12, 2001

The suicide bombings have increased. There's too many of them.

Albuquerque, NM, Aug. 15, 2001

We need to counter the shockwave of the evildoer by having individual rate cuts accelerated and by thinking about tax rebates [huh?].

Oct. 4, 2001

The problem with the French is that they don't have a word for "entrepreneur".

Washington Post, July 10, 2002

First, let me make it very clear, poor people aren't necessarily killers. Just because you happen to be not rich doesn't mean you're willing to kill.

May 19, 2003

This very week in 1989, there were protests in East Berlin and in Leipzig. By the end of that year, every communist dictatorship in Central America had collapsed.

Nov. 6, 2003

The march to war hurt the economy. Laura reminded me a while ago that remember what was on the TV screens— she calls me, "George W."— "George W." I call her, "First Lady". No, anyway—she said, we said, "March to war on our TV screen".

Bay Shore, New York, Mar. 11, 2004

And they [the Iraqi people] were happy—they're not happy they're occupied. I wouldn't be happy if I were occupied either.

Apr. 13, 2004

The CIA laid out several scenarios and said life could be lousy, life could be OK, life could be better, and they were just guessing as to what the conditions might be like.

New York, Sept. 21, 2004

I believe we are called to do the hard work to make our communities and quality of life a better place.

Collinsville, IL, Jan. 5, 2005

It's in our country's interests to find those who would do harm to us and get them out of harm's way.

Apr. 28, 2005

Now, I know people want things done tomorrow—or yesterday—and if they're not done, they say, "Well, the thing has fallen apart".

May 31, 2005

Stating the Obvious

There is a lot of speculation and I guess there is going to continue to be a lot of speculation until the speculation ends.

Austin American-Statesman, Oct. 18, 1998

I think we agree—the past is over.

Dallas Morning News, May 10, 2000

I think—I think the—the life issue is an issue.

Hardball, MSNBC, May 31, 2000

States should have the right to enact reasonable laws and restrictions, particularly to end the inhumane practice of ending a life that otherwise could live.

Washington Post, June 28, 2000

Well, maybe we ought—maybe we ought—I don't know the figure of one percent or 99 percent, but if that—if it's good public policy, it's good public policy.

Larry King Live, CNN, July 20, 2000

A key to foreign policy is to rely on reliance.

Washington Post, Nov. 1, 2000

And as far as what the legislature does in Florida, that's going to be up to the leadership in the legislature.

Dec. 4, 2000

Dick Cheney and I do not want this nation to be in a recession. We want anybody who can find work to be able to find work.

60 Minutes II, Dec. 5, 2000

More and more of our imports come from overseas.

Beaverton, OR, Sept. 25, 2000

And so, I hope investors, you know—secondly, I hope investors hold investments for periods of time—that I've always found the best investments are those that you salt away based on economics.

Austin, TX, Jan. 4, 2001

I'm hopeful. I know there is a lot of ambition in Washington, obviously. But I hope the ambitious realize that they are more likely to succeed with success as opposed to failure.

Jan. 18, 2001

Home is important. It's important to have a home.

Crawford, Feb. 18, 2001

It's very important for folks to understand that when there's more trade, there's more commerce.

Quebec City, Apr. 21, 2001

Our nation must come together to unite.

Tampa, FL, June 4, 2001

I understand that the unrest in the Middle East creates unrest throughout the region.

Mar. 13, 2002

We'll take two questions a side. We would hope that you would respect asking one question per question.

Mar. 27, 2003

Now, there are some who would like to rewrite history—"revisionist historians" is what I like to call them.

Elizabeth, N.J., June 16, 2003

And so I want to thank you [the Detroit Pistons] for setting an example of serving people who hurt. In other words, you have taken your great championship status and converted it to good. And that's good.

Jan 31, 2005

There's not doubt in my mind, when all is said and done, the facts will show the world the truth.

Sept. 20, 2005

Listen, I readily concede there is this attitude in Washington where, we can't work together because one party may benefit and the other party may not benefit. The people don't like that. They don't like that attitude. They expect members of both parties to come together to solve problems.

May 31, 2005

Oftentimes, Bushes use of the obvious seems so inexplicably awkward that one is left to wonder whether his use of a word in a proposition is not merely his repeating something out loud so as to commit a new word to memory, just as children do. Two such examples follow.

Now, by the way, "surplus" means a little money left over—otherwise it wouldn't be called "surplus".

Oct. 27, 2000

> [A]s you know, these are "open forums" — you're able to come and listen to what I have to say.
>
> Oct. 28, 2003

Here Bush responds to the Amnesty International charge that the U.S. treatment of prisoners around the world has taken the form of a "new gulag".

> It seemed like to me they based some of their decisions on the word of—and the allegations—by people who were held in detention, people who hate America, people that had been trained in some instances to disassemble [*sic*]—that means not tell the truth.
>
> May 31, 2005

Dubya the Philosopher

In spite of his disdain for books and his admission that he's not very analytical, Bush at times—not often, but at times—becomes a bit philosophical. Here he speaks philosophically to the University of Nebraska women's volleyball team, who were national champions in 2001.

> If a person doesn't have the capacity that we all want that person to have, I suspect hope is in the far distant future, if at all.
>
> May 22, 2001

> It's important for young men and women who look at the Nebraska champs to understand that quality of life is more than just blocking shots.
>
> May 31, 2001

> There's nothing more deep than recognizing Israel's right to exist. That's the most deep [*sic*] thought of all.... I can't think of anything more deep [*sic*] than that right.
>
> Mar. 13, 2002

> I'm also not very analytical. You know I don't spend a lot of time thinking about myself, about why I do things.
>
> June 4, 2003

The Post:	Do you plan to expend any political capital to aggressively lobby senators for a gay marriage amendment?
Bush:	You know, I think that the situation in the last session—well, first of all, I do believe it's necessary; many in the Senate didn't, because they believe DOMA [the Defense of Marriage Act] will—is in place, but—they know DOMA is in place, and they're waiting to see whether or not DOMA will withstand a constitutional challenge.
The Post:	Do you plan on trying to—using the White House, using the bully pulpit, and trying to—
Bush:	The point is—is that senators have made it clear that so long as DOMA is deemed constitutional, nothing will happen. I'd take their admonition seriously.
The Post:	But until that changes, you want it?
Bush:	Well, until that changes, nothing will happen in the Senate. Do you see what I'm saying?
The Post:	Right.
Bush:	The logic?

Washington Post, Jan. 16, 2005

Asking the Right Questions

The important question is, "How many hands have I shaked?"

New York Times, Oct. 23, 1999

Rarely is the question asked, "Is our children learning?"

Florence, S.C., Jan. 11, 2000

Will the highways on the Internet become more few?

Concord, NH, Jan. 29, 2000

The fundamental question is, "Will I be a successful president when it comes to foreign policy?" I will be, but until I'm the president, it's going to be hard for me to verify that I think I'll be more effective.

New York Times, June 28, 2000

To Brazilian President Fernando Cardoso, Bush asked the following penetrating question:

Do you have blacks, too?

Nov. 8, 2001

Now we're asking the question: "Show us".

North Virginia Community College, Aug. 9, 2004

I hope you leave here and walk out and say, "What did he say?"

Beaverton, Oregon, Aug. 13, 2004

If you're a younger person, you ought to be asking members of Congress and the United States Senate and the president what you intend to do about it. If you see a train wreck coming, you ought to be saying, "What are you going to do about it, Mr. Congressman or Madam Congressman?"

Detroit, Mich., Feb. 8, 2005

In this job you've got a lot on your plate on a regular basis; you don't have much time to sit around and wander, lonely, in the Oval Office, kind of asking different portraits, "How do you think my standing will be?"

Mar. 16, 2005

Who could have possibly envisioned an erection—an election in Iraq at this point in history?

D.C., Jan. 10, 2005

Occasionally—somebody proposed a law, for example, if you murder a pregnant woman, should the person be charged with murder once or twice?

Danish Broadcasting Corp., June 29, 2005

"Smooth" Recoveries!

The ambassador and the general were briefing me on the—the vast majority of Iraqis want to live in a peaceful, free world. And we will find these people and we will bring them to justice.

Oct. 27, 2003

And it's a relationship [with Russia], where it's complicated—it's complex, rather than complicated.

Dec. 20, 2004

Here two members of the *Washington Post* interview Bush and, when one introduces a "parochial question" (i.e., one relative to the D.C. area), the president takes this to be a criticism of terse answers.

The Post: A parochial question for *The Post* in D.C.
Bush: I'm trying to stay concentrated.
The Post: What's that?
Bush: I'm just trying to stay concentrated. You've got a whole—
The Post: I've got to ask you at least a couple domestic questions. Your answers are short, though.

Washington Post, Jan. 16, 2005

The Post: You used "partial privatization" yourself last year, sir.
Bush: Yes?
The Post: Yes, three times in one sentence. We had to figure this out, because we're in an argument with the RNC [Republican National Committee] about how we should actually word this. [*Post* staff writer] Mike Allen, the industrious Mike Allen, found it.
Bush: Allen did what now?
The Post: You used "partial privatization".
Bush: I did, personally?
The Post: Right.
Bush: When?
The Post: To describe it.
Bush: When—when was it?
The Post: Mike said it was right around the election.
Bush: Seriously?
The Post: It was right around the election. We'll send it over.
Bush: I'm surprised. Maybe I did. It's amazing what happens when you're tired. Anyway, your question was? I'm sorry for interrupting.

Washington Post, Jan 16, 2005

You work three jobs? Uniquely American, isn't it? I mean, that is fantastic that you're doing that.

Omaha, Nebraska, Feb. 4, 2005

The other thing is, is that it's clear from the other five parties there [in the coalition of nations dealing with North Korea's nuclear program]—the other four parties in our five-party coalition dealing with the sixth party, which is North Korea—is that people do want to solve this issue diplomatically.

May 31, 2005

The best way to convince Kim Jong-il to get up—give up his weapons is to have more than one voice saying the same thing.

May 31, 2005

Chapter 13
Bush: S to Z

"Alice was beginning to get very tired of sitting by her sister on the bank, and of having nothing to do: once or twice she had peeped into the book her sister was reading, but it had no pictures or conversations in it, 'and what is the use of a book', thought Alice, 'without pictures or conversations?'"

Revealing Slips

I'm trying to protect my invest—, my contributors from unscrupulous practices.

Houston Chronicle, July 18, 1998

I don't care what the polls say. I don't. I'm doing what I think what's wrong.

New York Times, Mar. 15, 2000

The only thing that I can tell you is that every case I have reviewed, I have been comfortable with the innocence or guilt of the person that I've looked at. I do not believe we've put a guilty—I mean—innocent person to death in the state of Texas.

All Things Considered, NPR, June 16, 2000

> The best way to relieve families from time is to let them keep some of their own money.
>
> Westminster, CA, Sept. 13, 2000

> I'm the one—when I put my hand on the Bible, when I put my hand on the Bible, that day when they swear us in, when I put my hand on the Bible—I will swear to not—to uphold the laws of the land.
>
> Toledo, Oct. 27, 2000

> I want everybody to hear loud and clear that I'm going to be the president of everybody.
>
> Jan. 18, 2001

> I appreciate that question because I, in the state of Texas, had heard a lot of discussion about a faith-based initiative eroding the important bridge between church and state.
>
> Jan. 29, 2001

> First, we would not accept a treaty that would not have been ratified, nor a treaty that I thought made sense for the country.
>
> Apr. 24, 2001

> My administration has been calling upon all the leaders in the—in the Middle East to do everything they can to stop the violence, to tell the different parties involved that peace will never happen.
>
> Crawford, TX, Aug, 13, 2001

> And this is a new kind of evil—and we understand, and the American people are beginning to understand, this crusade, this war on terrorism, is going to take a while, and the American people must be patient.
>
> Sept. 16, 2001

The word "crusade", of course, brought back memories of the Catholic crusaders who fought the Muslims from 1096 to 1271. He used the same word once again on February 16 of 2002, while in Alaska.

> We are resolved to rout out terror wherever it exists to save the world from freedom.
>
> Atlanta, Jan. 31, 2002

Here Bush addresses the people in Austin who've come to see the unveiling and hanging of a new portrait of himself.

I want to thank you for taking time out of your day to come and witness my hanging.

Austin, TX, Jan. 4, 2002

Not over my dead body will they raise your taxes.

Ontario, CA, Jan. 5, 2002

It would be a mistake for the United States Senate to allow any kind of human cloning to come out of that chamber.

Apr. 10, 2002

You're free. And freedom is beautiful. And, you know, it'll take time to restore chaos and order—order out of chaos. But we will.

Apr. 13, 2003

All up and down the different aspects of our society, we had meaningful discussions. Not only in the Cabinet Room, but prior to this and after this day, our secretaries, respective secretaries, will continue to interact to create the conditions necessary for prosperity to reign.

May 19, 2003

[T]hat's just the nature of democracy. Sometimes pure politics enters into the rhetoric.

Crawford, TX, Aug. 8, 2003

We're still being challenged in Iraq and the reason why is a free Iraq will be a major defeat in the cause of freedom.

Charlotte, N.C., Apr. 5, 2004

Our enemies are innovative and resourceful, and so are we. They never stop thinking about new ways to harm our country and our people, and neither do we.

Aug. 5, 2004

In a changing world, we want more people to have control over your own life.

Annandale, VA, Aug. 9, 2004

There's no doubt in my mind that we should allow the world worst leaders to hold America hostage, to threaten our peace, to threaten our friends and allies with the world's worst weapons.

South Bend, IN, Sept. 5, 2002

We will make sure our troops have all that is necessary to complete their missions. That's why I went to the Congress last September and proposed fundamental—supplemental funding, which is money for armor and body parts and ammunition and fuel.

Erie, PA, Sept. 4, 2004

But to say that there's only one focus on the war on terror doesn't really understand the nature of the war on terror. Of course we're after Saddam Hussein—I mean bin Laden.

Bush/Kerry I, Sept. 30, 2004

My opponent just said something amazing. He said Osama bin Laden uses the invasion of Iraq as an excuse to spread hatred for America. Osama bin Laden isn't going to determine how we defend ourselves. Osama bin Laden doesn't get to decide. The American people decide. *I* decided the right action was in Iraq.

Bush/Kerry I, Sept. 30, 2004

The truth of that matter is, if you listen carefully, Saddam would still be in power if he were the president of the United States, and the world would be a lot better off.

Bush/Kerry II, Oct. 8, 2004

Russert: But can you launch a pre-emptive war without iron-clad, absolute intelligence that he had weapons of mass destruction?

Bush: Let me take a step back for a second and—there is no such thing necessarily *in a dictatorial regime* of iron-clad absolutely solid evidence. The evidence I had was the best possible evidence that he had a weapon.

Meet the Press, Feb. 7, 2004

This notion that the United States is getting ready to attack Iran is simply ridiculous. And having said that, all options are on the table.

Brussels, Belgium, Feb. 22, 2005

I—you probably suffered through this part of my speech on the campaign a lot when I talked about my relationship with Koizumi [of Japan].

May 31, 2005

Tongue-Tied

I understand. I understand, but the point I say to you is—is that you know—if what you're suggesting is—is that—what I'm suggesting to you is if you can't name the foreign minister of Mexico, therefore—you know—you're not capable of what you do. But the truth of the matter is—you're—is—you are—whether you can or not.

Nov. 4, 1999

If he's—the inference is that somehow he thinks slavery is a—is a noble institution I would—I would strongly reject that assumption—that John Ashcroft is a open-minded, [*sic*] inclusive person.

Jan. 14, 2001

It's good to see so many friends here in the Rose Garden. This is our first event in this beautiful spot, and it's appropriate we talk about policy that will affect people's lives in a positive way in such a beautiful, beautiful part of our national—our national—really, our national park system, I guess, is you'd want to call it.

Feb. 8, 2001

There's a lot of people in the Middle East who are desirous to get into the Mitchell process [i.e. George Mitchell's plan for Middle East peace]. And—but first things first. The—these terrorist acts and, you know, the responses have got to end in order for us to get the framework—the groundwork, not framework—the groundwork to discuss a framework for peace, to lay the—all right.

Crawford, TX, Aug.13, 2001

And then there's this absolutely inappropriate comment on the first plane crash of 9/11.

And it—I was sitting outside the—the classroom, waiting to go in, and I saw an airplane hit the tower of a—of a—you know, the TV was obviously on, and I—I used to fly myself, and I said, "Well, there's one terrible pilot!"

Dec. 4, 2001

And so, in my State of the—my State of the Union—or state—my speech to the nation, whatever you want to call it, speech to the nation—I asked Americans to give 4,000 years—4,000 hours over the next—the rest of your life—of service to America. That's what I asked—4,000 hours.

Bridgeport, CN, Apr. 9, 2002

There's an old saying in Tennessee—I know it's in Texas, probably in Tennessee—that says, fool me once, shame on—shame on you. Fool me—you can't get fooled again.

Nashville, TN, Sept. 17, 2002

I think the American people—I hope the American—I don't think, let me—I hope the American people trust me.

Dec 18, 2002

Secondly, the tactics of our—as you know, we don't have relationships with Iran. I mean, that's—ever since the late '70s, we have no contacts with them, and we've totally sanctioned them. In other words, there's no sanctions [*sic*]—you can't—we're out of sanctions.

Annandale, VA, Aug. 9, 2004

Having said that—no, no, I understand completely. Look, what we're going to do is we're going to have government—look, the world has changed.

Phone Interview with Rush Limbaugh, Aug. 31, 2004

See, once they hear from the people, we got a problem, the next—the next question the people—question the people are going to ask, what do you intend to do about it?

May 31, 2005

But from that point going forward [on the stem-cell issue], I felt it was best to stand on principle—and that is taxpayers' money to use—for the use—for the use of experimentation that would destroy life is a principle that violates something I—I mean, is a position that violates a principle of mine.

May 31, 2005

Untidy Metaphors

We ought to make the pie higher.

GOP Debate, SC, Feb. 15, 2000

The senator [McCain] has got to understand if he's going to have—he can't have it both ways. He can't take the high horse and then claim the low road.

Florence, SC, Feb. 17, 2000

We want our teachers to be trained so they can meet the obligations—their obligations as teachers. We want them to know how to teach the science of reading. In order to make sure there's not this kind of federal—federal cufflink.

Milwaukee, Mar. 30, 2000

I hope we get to the bottom of the answer. It's what I'm interested to know.

Associated Press, Apr. 26, 2000

Families is [*sic*] where our nation finds hope, where wings take dream.

LaCrosse, WI, Oct. 18, 2000

It's important for us to explain to our nation that life is important. It's not only life of babies, but it's life of children living in, you know, the dark dungeons of the Internet.

Arlington Heights, IL, Oct. 24, 2000

It's hard for me to put myself in anybody else's shoes about their personal lives. All I can tell you is it's made my life better and easier to understand, and clearer. It's made my walk clearer. And I emphasize the walk because life's journey is, you know, there's pitfalls [*sic*] and there's challenges [*sic*].

Beliefnet.com, 2000

We'll be a great country where the fabrics are made up of groups and loving centers.

Kalamazoo, MI, Mar. 27, 2001

Sometimes, Washington is one of these towns where the person—people who think they've got the sharp elbow is the most effective person.

New Orleans, Dec. 3, 2002

The doctrine of containment just doesn't hold any water, as far as I'm concerned.

Feb. 23, 2003

Perhaps one way will be, if we use military force, in the post-Saddam Iraq the U.N. will definitely need to have a role. And that way it can begin to get its legs, legs of responsibility back.

The Azores, Portugal, Mar. 16, 2003

Security is the essential roadblock to achieving the road map to peace.

July 25, 2003

Free societies are hopeful societies. And free societies will be allies against these hateful few who have no conscience, who kill at the whim of a hat.

Sept. 17, 2004

You can run but you can't hide the reality.

Bush/Kerry II, Oct. 8, 2004

A couple of more [questions], then I got to hop. Keith. I get to leave. That's not a very—a couple of more, and then I have to retire, as opposed to hopping.

May 31, 2005

Verbal Valetudinarian

I know how hard it is for you to put food on your family.

Greater Nashua, NH, Jan. 27, 2000

A reformer with results is a conservative who has had compassionate results in the state of Texas.

New York Times, Feb. 10, 2000

I understand small business growth. I was one.

New York Daily News, Feb. 19, 2000

We're concerned about AIDS inside our White House—make no mistake about it.

Feb. 7, 2001

Africa is a nation, [*sic*] that suffers from incredible disease.

June 14, 2001

I'm a proud man to be the nation based upon such wonderful values.

July 2, 2001

Over 75 percent of white Americans own their home, and less than 50 percent of Hispanos [*sic*] and African Americans don't own their home. And that's a gap—that's a homeownership gap. And we've got to do something about it.

Cleveland, July 1, 2002

I've got very good relations with President Mubarak and Crown Prince Abdallah and the King of Jordan, Gulf Coast countries.

May 29, 2003

We are making steadfast progress.

June 9, 2003

It's very interesting when you think about it, the slaves who left here to go to America, because of their steadfast and their religion and their belief in freedom, helped change America.

Dakar, Senegal, July 8, 2003

We had a chance to visit with Teresa Nelson who's a parent, and a mom or a dad.

Jacksonville, Florida, Sept. 9, 2003

[W]hether they be Christian, Jew, or Muslim, or Hindu, people have heard the universal call to love a neighbor just like they'd like to be called themselves.

Oct. 8, 2003

So thank you for reminding me about the importance of being a good mom and a great volunteer as well.

St. Louis, Jan. 5, 2004

> I want to thank my friend, Senator Bill Frist, for joining us today. You're doing a heck of a job. You cut your teeth here, right? That's where you started practicing? That's good. He married a Texas girl, I want you to know. Karyn is with us. A West Texas girl—just like me.
>
> Nashville, TN, May 27, 2004

> She [Hillary Clinton] has proven herself more equal [*sic*] to the challenge [of the US Senate].
>
> June 14, 2004

> The enemy understands a free Iraq will be a major defeat in their ideology of hatred. That's why they're fighting so vociferously.
>
> Bush/Kerry I, Sept. 30, 2004

> It's a time of sorrow and sadness when we lose a loss of life.
>
> Dec. 21, 2004

> And so during these holiday seasons, we thank our blessings.
>
> Fort Belvoir, Va., Dec. 10, 2004

> We are in no way, shape, or form should a human being play God.
>
> *20/20*, Jan. 14, 2005

> I'm going to spend a lot of time on Social Security. I enjoy it. I enjoy taking on the issue. I guess it's the mother in me.
>
> April 14, 2005

When asked about the U.S.'s "scrapping" of the program to return home those bodies of soldiers killed in the Korean War, Bush replies with typical verbal dexterity:

> The Secretary of Defense decided to take a—what he's referring to is, is that we have—I wouldn't called it "scrapped"—is that the verb you used? "Scrapped"? [The reporter responds affirmatively.] Yes, "scrapped". I would use a different verb. I would use "reassess" the mission. See, "scrapped" means that we're not going to do it ever again, I think is what that means. And what the Secretary of Defense has said, "Let me just take a look and make sure that as we send people into North Korea, that we're fully mindful of them being able to go in and get out". "No immediate threat, just an assessment", is how I would put it. But thank you for the question.

It's a Dangerous World!

This is still a dangerous world. It's a world of madmen and uncertainty and potential mental losses.

Financial Times, Jan. 14, 2000

When I was coming up, it was a dangerous world, and you know exactly who they were. It was us versus them, and it was clear who them was. Today, we are not so sure who the "they" are, but we know they're there.

Iowa Western Community College, Jan. 21, 2000

My point is, is that I want America to lead the nation—lead the world—toward a more safe world when it comes to nuclear weaponry.

New York Times, Jan. 27, 2000

I think we ought to raise the age at which juveniles can have a gun.

Bush/Gore III, Oct. 17, 2000

For every fatal shooting, there were roughly three non-fatal shootings. And, folks, this is unacceptable in America. It's just unacceptable. And we're going to do something about it.

Philadelphia, May 14, 2001

When they struck, they wanted to create an atmosphere of fear. And one of the great goals of this nation's war is to restore public confidence in the airline industry. It's to tell the traveling public: "Get on board. Do your business around the country. Fly and enjoy America's great destination spots. Get down to Disney World in Florida. Take your families and enjoy life, the way we want it to be enjoyed".

Sept. 27, 2001

Yes, I can't put it any more plainly, Iraq is a dangerous place. That's leveling. It is a dangerous place.... And Iraq is dangerous, and it's dangerous because terrorists want us to leave. And we're not leaving.

Oct. 28, 2003

Justice was being delivered to a man who defied that gift from the Almighty to the people of Iraq.

Dec. 15, 2003

Xenial Ambassador

Welcome. It's my honor to welcome the Prime Minister [Tony Blair], from our strongest friend and closest ally, to Camp David. We've had a couple of formal visits; more importantly, had a nice walk around Camp David, and got to know each other. And as they told me, he's a pretty charming guy. He put the charm offensive on me. (Yucks.) And it worked.

Camp David, Feb. 23, 2001

Bush:	Thank you for the beautiful weather.
Kwasniewski:	We have special relations. (Yucks.)
Bush:	I'll try to highlight that in my speech this afternoon. (More yucks.)

Warsaw, June 15, 2001

It's my honor to speak to you [new immigrants to the U.S.] as the leader of your country. And the great thing about America is you don't have to listen unless you want to.

July 10, 2001

You saw the president yesterday. I thought he was very forward-leaning, as they say in diplomatic nuanced circles.

July 23, 2001

Border relations between Canada and Mexico [*sic*] have never been better.

Press Conference with Jean Chretien, Sept. 24, 2001

My trip to Asia begins here in Japan for an important reason. It begins here because for a century and a half now [*sic*], America and Japan have formed one of the great and enduring alliances of modern times. From that alliance has come an era of peace in the Pacific.

Tokyo, Feb. 18, 2002

This foreign policy stuff is a little frustrating.

New York Daily News, Apr. 23, 2002

I consider Vladimir Putin one of my good friends. Are you going to translate. (Yucks.) Like other good friends, I've had throughout my life, we don't agree 100 percent of the time. But we always agree to discuss things in a frank and—in a frank way.

St. Petersburg, Oct 22, 2002

I'm not the expert on how the Iraqi people think, because I live in America, where it's nice and safe and secure.

Sept. 23, 2004

The president [Ricardo Lagos] and I also reaffirmed our determination to fight terror, to bring drug trafficking to bear, to bring justice to those who pollute our youth.

Santiago, Chile, Nov. 21, 2004

The following recent bit of diplomacy occurred when, in a joint press conference, a question is asked first of President Abbas of Palestine and then of Bush. Bush replies first and then, forgetting about Abbas, fields another question.

Bush: ...And we continue to remind our friends, the Israelis, about their obligations under the road map, just like we remind President Abbas about the obligations under the road map that the Palestinians have accepted. So nothing has changed.
Adam, yes.... Oh, I'm sorry. I beg your pardon.

Abbas: The first one.

Bush: I beg your—sorry, yes. Just trying to cut you off. (Yucks.) It's an old Rose Garden trick.

May 26, 2005

Presidential Yapping

Yapping is slang for idle or foolish talking. Bush, of course, does more than his share of this.

When asked if he knew anything about Vladimir Putin, the new Russian leader, Bush replied:

I really don't. I will if I'm the president.

Meet the Press, Nov. 21, 1999

I've been consistent throughout the course of the campaign that my Supreme Court will be people that will not use the bench from which to legislate.

USA Today, Nov. 3, 2000

The legislature's job is to write law. It's the executive branch's job to interpret law.

Austin, TX, Nov. 22, 2000

The person who runs FEMA is someone who must have the trust of the president. Because the person who runs FEMA is the first voice, often times, of someone whose life has been turned upside down hears from.

Austin, TX, Jan. 4, 2001

The California crunch really is the result of not enough power-generating plants and then not enough power to power the power of generating plants.

Jan. 14, 2001

We want to develop defenses that are capable of defending ourselves and defenses capable of defending others.

Mar. 29, 2001

Anyway, I'm so thankful, and so gracious—I'm gracious that my brother Jeb is concerned about the hemisphere as well.

June 4, 2001

I haven't had a chance to talk, but I'm confident we'll get a bill that I can live with, if we don't.

June 13, 2001

It's negative to think about blowing each other up. That's not a positive thought.

Wall Street Journal, June 25, 2001

[W]e now understand one plus one can equal three, as opposed to us and Russia we hope to be zero.

Nov. 15, 2001

The trial lawyers are very politically powerful.... But here in Texas we took them on and got some good medical—medical malpractice.

Waco, TX, Aug. 13, 2002

Washington is a town where there's all kinds [*sic*] of allegations. You've heard much of the allegations. And if people have got solid information, please come forward with it. And that would be people inside the information who are the so-called "anonymous sources", or people outside the information—outside the administration.

Chicago, Sept. 30, 2003

My views are one that speaks to freedom.

Jan. 29, 2004

I always jest to people, the Oval Office is the kind of place where people stand outside, they're getting ready to come in and tell me what for, and they walk in and get overwhelmed in the atmosphere, and they say, "Man, you're looking pretty".

Nov. 4, 2004

We've got a lot of work to do with the North Korean because he—he tends to ignore what the other five nations are saying at times. But that doesn't mean we're going to stop, and continue to press forward to making it clear that if he expects to be treated as a responsible nation, that he needs to listen to the five nations involved.

May 31, 2005

Here, Bush graciously calls on reporter Matt Cooper so that he can "resonate" around the country.

Matt Cooper. Here we go—no, go with the mic, Matt. We want you heard. We want you resonating around the country.

May 31, 2005

Zany Modalities

The great thing about America is everybody should vote.

Austin, TX, Dec. 8, 2000

I am mindful not only of preserving executive powers for myself, but for predecessors as well.

Jan. 29, 2001

There's no question that the minute I got elected, the storm clouds on the horizon were getting nearly directly overhead.

May 11, 2001

Saddam Hussein is a man who told the world he wouldn't have weapons of mass destruction, but he's got them.

Apr. 30, 2002

> I promise you I will listen to what has been said here, even though I wasn't here.
>
> Waco, TX, Aug. 13, 2002

> I love the idea of a school in which people come to get educated and stay in the state in which they're educated.
>
> Milwaukee, WI, Aug. 14, 2002

> One year ago today, the time for excuse-making has come to an end.
>
> Jan. 8, 2003

> Iran would be dangerous if they have a nuclear weapon.
>
> June 18, 2003

> I know the Iraqi people don't believe that, that they're better off with Saddam Hussein—would be better off with Saddam Hussein in power.
>
> Apr. 13, 2004

> My job is to, like, think beyond the immediate.
>
> Apr. 21, 2004

> Bill Davidson. I've known Bill Davidson in the past, he is a true gentleman, a great civic leader in the Detroit area.
>
> Congratulating the Detroit Pistons, Jan. 31, 2005

Bush reminds a reporter below that he did in fact express concern in a prior address with President Abbas about the anti-democratic tactics in the recent elections in Egypt. The claim Bush makes is that when he did express concern he was perhaps not quite as articulate as he was when he did expressed concern!

> Pretty confident I said that with President Abbas standing here—maybe not quite as articulately as just then.
>
> May 31, 2005

> I look forward to talking to members of the Senate about the Supreme Court process to get their opinions, as well, and will do so—and will do so.
>
> May 31, 2005

Afterward
Where Do We Go From Here?

"It seems a shame", the Walrus said,
"To play them such a trick,
After we've brought them out so far,
And made them trot so quick!"
The Carpenter said nothing but
"The butter's spread too thick!"

ALL OF US KNOW THE CONCLUSION to the story of Alice. She wakes to find that Hatter and Hare, Mock Turtle and Gryphon, Walrus and Carpenter were merely part of a long, wild, and "curious" dream. What are we to make of America's present conundrum? Is it too a long, wild, and "curious", but nightmarish sort of dream, from which we may someday hope to wake?

Of course, those of us who recognize the danger may hope at some point that a scandal, sufficiently large to expose the deep-rooted corruption in the administration, may pop up and force substantial changes through widespread public dissent. This, though, seems unlikely, as news of deceit, lies, dissimulation, and corruption in the administration has been accessible to the American public for years now and has generated astonishingly little dissent. Most recently, what comes to mind are the Valerie Plame/Karl Rove affair and the Downing-Street-Memos scandal that have had little effect on the U.S. public.

Americans—placated continually by spoon-fed lines like "It's hard work" and "We're making progress"—seem content merely to stay the course, while ignoring the opposition of the rest of the world that fears an imperialistic agenda.

Why have Americans been reluctant to act or even voice their dissent with the present administration? It is, I presume, because they have recognized neither the full extent of the danger nor the wickedness of the administration. Without full recognition of a problem, there isn't sufficient reason for remedial action.

Yet the war in Iraq drags on, without end in sight. Casualties mount on both sides. Thousands of U.S. soldiers have already lost their lives; many more will be lost in the months, perhaps years, to come. Billions of borrowed dollars are being pumped into the "reconstruction" of Iraq. There is always the hope of a reasonable return on this "investment" of lost lives and borrowed money in the years ahead, but as the war drags on, this hope too seems baseless. When will the fighting end? Americans again hear the careworn sentence, "As the Iraqis stand up, we will stand down".

With the recent devastation of Hurricane Katrina and the meteoric rise of fuel prices thereafter, Bush's approval rating, as high as 90 percent after 9/11, has plummeted as low as 38 percent. In an address on September 12 of 2005 in New Orleans, many days after Hurricane Katrina, Bush deflected a reporter's suggestion that his own "management style" might have been in part responsible for the government's slow response to the thousands of helpless, stranded people in the flooded city. "Look, there will be plenty of time to play the blame game", he said. He added shortly, "Now, as far as my own personal popularity goes, I don't make decisions based on polls".

Back in Washington one day later, a frustrated George W. Bush—the president who never makes decisions "based on polls"—attempted to do something at a press conference that he had never before done as president: assume responsibility.

> Katrina exposed serious problems in our response capability at all levels of government. And to the extent that the federal government didn't fully do its job right, *I take responsibility.* I want to know what went right and what went wrong. I want to know how to better cooperate [*sic*] with state and local government, to be able to answer that very question that you asked: Are we capable of dealing with a severe attack or another severe storm?

Of course, there was the qualifying, "to the extent that the federal government didn't fully do its job right…", which left open the possibility that the federal government *did* fully do its job right. There's always an "out" for Bush. Qualifier notwithstanding, it must have been painful for him to say those three words that followed: "I take responsibility".

Polls do matter. Bush is abundantly aware of this. Just what do these polls say? As of this writing, almost two-thirds of Americans (63%) favor some sort of troop withdrawal in Iraq. Most (59%) believe the war was a mistake and almost as many Americans (58%) believe he (i.e., his reelection) was a mistake. Carroll Doherty of the Pew Research Center recently said, "Bush stands at a precipice. He's lost ground among independents. He seems to be starting to lose ground among his own party. And he lost the Democrats a long time ago".[1] Maybe, just maybe, the American public is beginning to get fed up. Perhaps they too, like young Alice, shall shortly wake from their "curious" dream.

---

1 Susan Page, "Bush's Ratings Hit Record Low, Poll Says", *USA Today*, http://www.indystar.com/apps/pbcs.dll/article?AID=/20050920/NEWS06/509200451/1012.

Author Biography

Dr. M. Andrew Holowchak is an Assistant Professor of Philosophy at Kutztown University, near Allentown. His research interests are mainly in the areas of Ancient Philosophy (esp. ethics), Philosophy of Science, Critical Reasoning, and Freudian Psychoanalysis. He enjoys writing and has published nearly thirty papers in areas such as ethics, ancient philosophy, and social and political philosophy and has authored several books including *Happiness and Greek Ethics, Critical Reasoning & Philosophy,* and *Ancient Science and Dreams: Oneirology in Greco-Roman Antiquity.*

When not teaching or writing, Holowchak enjoys strength training (former super-heavyweight power-lifting champion), biking, gardening, travel, and polite conversation. He currently lives in Macungie, Pennsylvania, with his fiancée, Angela.

www.ingramcontent.com/pod-product-compliance
Ingram Content Group UK Ltd.
Pitfield, Milton Keynes, MK11 3LW, UK
UKHW041828200726
13854UKWH00002BA/654